# A Very Merry Christmas Cookbook

# A Very Merry Christmas Cookbook

By *the* Editors *of*
Good Housekeeping

HEARST BOOKS
*A Division of*
STERLING PUBLISHING CO., INC.
NEW YORK

GOOD HOUSEKEEPING

| | |
|---|---|
| Ellen Levine | Editor in Chief |
| Susan Westmoreland | Food Director |
| Susan Deborah Goldsmith | Associate Food Director |
| Delia Hammock | Nutrition Director |
| Sharon Franke | Food Appliances Director |
| Richard Eisenberg | Special Projects Director |

BOOK DESIGN: DEBORAH KERNER/DANCING BEARS DESIGN

Library of Congress Cataloging-in-Publication Data

Good Housekeeping a very merry Christmas cookbook / by the editors of Good Housekeeping.
    p. cm.
  ISBN 1-58816-282-6
  1. Christmas cookery. 2. Entertaining. I. Good Housekeeping Institute (New York, N.Y.)
  TX739.2.C45G65 2003
  641.5'68--dc21                            2003001535

10 9 8 7 6 5 4 3

First Paperback Edition 2003

Published by Hearst Books
A Division of Sterling Publishing Co., Inc.
387 Park Avenue South, New York, NY 10016

The Good Housekeeping Cookbook Seal guarantees that the recipes in this cookbook meet the strict standards of the Good Housekeeping Institute, a source of reliable information and a consumer advocate since 1900. Every recipe has been triple-tested for ease, reliability, and great taste.

www.goodhousekeeping.com

For information about custom editions, special sales, premium and corporate purchases, please contact Sterling Special Sales Department at 800-805-5489 or specialsales@sterlingpub.com.

Distributed in Canada by Sterling Publishing
℅ Canadian Manda Group, 165 Dufferin Street
Toronto, Ontario, Canada M6K 3H6

Distributed in Australia by Capricorn Link (Australia) Pty. Ltd.
P.O. Box 704, Windsor, NSW 2756 Australia

Manufactured in China

Sterling ISBN 13: 978-1-58816-514-5
     ISBN 10: 1-58816-514-0

# Contents

# Foreword

The countdown to the winter holidays starts early at *Good Housekeeping*—we're already thinking about the following year soon after New Year's Day. Preparing for this joyous season is a tradition we cherish and enjoy—and take seriously. We loved the idea of a book that could help you entertain—and that's how *Good Housekeeping A Very Merry Christmas Cookbook* was born.

We know it's not easy to put together a memorable celebration filled with great food and beautiful centerpieces. Like you, we're guided by thoughts of family and love, hallmarks of the *Good Housekeeping* tradition, and we have a practical bent as well: planning menus, making lists of necessary ingredients, and sharing ideas for table decorations.

In my family, the classics are the most rewarding at the holidays: delicious dishes passed down through the generations, mouthwatering cookies that remain tempting year after year, and traditional table centerpieces that are always elegant. We hope these pages filled with our favorite recipes will become your favorites as well. And let me know about your family's traditions, with all the trimmings!

In a season filled with joy, I wish you a healthy, fun-filled, beautiful holiday.

—ELLEN LEVINE
EDITOR IN CHIEF,
*Good Housekeeping*

# Introduction

The magic of Christmas suggests cherished traditions and beloved rituals shared with family and friends. But the party planning and cooking can sometimes seem too much to handle. That's why it's helpful to have expert guidance when organizing the perfect holiday meal.

We at *Good Housekeeping* can provide just that assistance in *A Very Merry Christmas Cookbook*: all you need for a festive holiday updated for today's lifestyle. As you thumb through these pages, you'll see how you can create magic with our triple-tested, irresistible recipes and lovely, easy-to-make centerpieces.

Celebrate with your guests and tantalize their appetites with Christmas Quesadillas, Lacy Parmesan Crisps, and Caviar Pie. Serve a delectable entree like Pork Crown Roast with Apple Stuffing or Crispy Citrus Goose to a beaming family and guests. Keep time spent in the kitchen to a minimum with make-ahead side dishes like Sweet Potato and Apple Gratin or Green Beans with Honey-Pecan Butter. For the grand finale, choose a divinely delicious dessert, such as our luscious Tiramisu Cake or a stunning Brandied Bûche de Noël. And perhaps the best of all, *A Very Merry Christmas Cookbook* has cookies, cookies, and more cookies: Great Granny's Old-Time Spice Cookies, Peanutty Yummy Bars, Chocolate Sambuca Cookies, Cinnamon Twists, and Jelly Centers, to name a few.

We give you our best wishes and our favorite recipes to present a season of tasty treats and memorable entertaining. *A Very Merry Christmas Cookbook* will inspire and delight you. Enjoy the holiday season with the greatest of ease!

## A Note about Using the Nutritional Values in this Book

At the bottom of each recipe, you'll find nutritional information. These calculations do not include any optional ingredients or garnishes, and when alternative ingredients are given, such as margarine, the calculations are based on the first ingredient listed. Unless otherwise noted, whole milk has been used.

# Entertaining

Sharing the joy of the season with festive foods and sweet indulgences is as much a part of the celebration as the Christmas tree. Pick and choose among these best-ever holiday recipes to present a Yuletide feast or to entertain friends at a casual get-together. And so no one is left out, we've included a children's party theme. Here are a few tips.

♦ Lists are the easiest way to get organized. Have a master "To Do" list plus individual lists for specific tasks. When entertaining, always have a guest list, a menu list, and two shopping lists for nonperishable and perishable items.

♦ To avoid an exhausting last-minute rush of trying to get too many things done in too little time, set a schedule for completing as many tasks as possible in advance of the event.

♦ Start your holiday baking right after Thanksgiving. Many cookie doughs can be frozen for up to two months. Depending upon type, finished baked goods, when properly wrapped, can be frozen for one to three months.

♦ Early in December: Purchase nonperishable foodstuffs. Stock bar supplies, including soft drinks. Count chairs, glasses, serving dishes, and utensils; borrow, buy, or rent what you need.

♦ Complete as much of the food preparation ahead as possible. Many of the appetizers and side dishes in the following pages include do-ahead instructions.

♦ Be prepared for unexpected guests by stocking the pantry with savories for shortcut appetizers. Marinated artichokes, tapenade, fancy nuts, pâté, assorted cheeses, and crackers are great hurry-up hors d'oeuvres.

♦ Remember, this is the season of good cheer and fellowship. Relax and have fun!

# Appetizers

▲ CHRISTMAS
QUESADILLAS P.16

## Potato Nests

**Prep:** 45 minutes plus chilling ◆ **Bake:** 31 to 33 minutes
**Makes** 32 nests

1. In 3-quart saucepan, combine potatoes and enough *water* to cover; heat to boiling over high heat. Reduce heat; cover and simmer 20 minutes, or until potatoes are just cooked through. Drain potatoes; refrigerate about 1 hour or until chilled.

2. Meanwhile, in small bowl, mix sour cream, horseradish, and dill until blended. Cover and refrigerate until ready to serve.

3. Preheat oven to 425°F. Grease thirty-two 1¾" by 1" mini muffin-pan cups.

4. Peel and coarsely grate potatoes. In medium bowl, gently toss grated potatoes with salt and pepper. Place about 1 heaping measuring tablespoon potato mixture in each mini muffin-pan cup; press mixture against bottom and up sides of cups, allowing some mixture to extend slightly above rim.

5. Bake potato nests 25 minutes, or until edges are golden brown. Cover pans loosely with foil if nests brown too quickly. Cool nests in pans on wire rack 10 minutes. Carefully transfer potato nests to jelly-roll pan or cookie sheet lined with paper towels. Let stand at room temperature up to 4 hours before serving.

6. To serve, preheat oven to 375°F. Place nests on large cookie sheet (without paper towels), and bake 6 to 8 minutes, until heated through and

2 large baking potatoes
(1½ pounds), unpeeled
½ cup sour cream
1 tablespoon prepared white
horseradish
1 tablespoon chopped fresh dill
½ teaspoon salt
⅛ teaspoon ground black pepper
dill sprigs and/or smoked salmon
for topping (optional)
pepper slices and radish for
garnish

**Each filled nest without
topping:** About 20 calories,
0 g protein, 3 g carbohydrate,
1 g total fat (1 g saturated),
2 mg cholesterol, 40 mg sodium.

crisp. Transfer nests to platter. Spoon about 1 teaspoon sour-cream mixture into each nest, and top each with a dill sprig or a small piece of smoked salmon, if you like. Garnish plate with pepper slices and radish.

*Appetizers* are versatile tidbits that can be appetite teasers for the courses to follow or the makings of a whole meal. Allow 4 to 5 per guest when a meal is to follow, 10 to 12 when no other food will be served. So that guests can easily and neatly manage to hold and eat them, keep appetizers bite-size.

# Olive Twists

**Prep:** 30 minutes   ◆   **Bake:** 12 to 15 minutes per batch
**Makes** about 56 twists

1. Preheat oven to 400°F. In small bowl, with fork, mix feta cheese, parsley, olive paste, and egg whites until thoroughly blended; set aside.
2. On lightly floured surface, unfold 1 pastry sheet, keeping other sheet refrigerated. Using floured rolling pin, roll out pastry sheet into 16" by 14" rectangle. Cut pastry in half crosswise. Spread half of olive mixture evenly over 1 pastry half; top with remaining pastry half. Using rolling pin, gently roll over pastry layers to seal them together.
3. Grease large cookie sheet. With large chef's knife, cut pastry rectangle crosswise into ½-inch-wide strips, taking care not to tear pastry. Twist each strip 3 to 4 times, then place strips about 1 inch apart on cookie sheet.

1 package (8 ounces) feta cheese, well drained and crumbled
⅓ cup chopped fresh parsley
⅓ cup olive paste or ½ cup Kalamata olives, pitted and pureed with 1 tablespoon olive oil
2 large egg whites
1 package (17¼ ounces) frozen puff-pastry sheets, thawed

**Each twist:** About 55 calories, 1 g protein, 5 g carbohydrate, 4 g total fat (1 g saturated), 4 mg cholesterol, 80 mg sodium.

◀ *P*OTATO NESTS
◆

◀ *O*LIVE TWISTS
◆

4. Bake strips 12 to 15 minutes, until pastry is puffed and lightly browned. With wide spatula, transfer sticks to wire rack to cool. Repeat with remaining pastry sheet and olive mixture. Serve at room temperature. Store in tightly covered container.

# Pickled Vegetables

**Prep:** 30 minutes plus overnight to chill
**Makes** 12 first-course servings

2 bags (16 ounces each) carrots, peeled and cut into 4" by ¼" matchstick strips
1 pound green beans, trimmed
1 medium head cauliflower (2 pounds), separated into flowerets
1 small bunch celery, cut into 4" by ½" matchstick strips
3 cups cider vinegar
⅓ cup sugar
2 teaspoons salt
1 cup water
1 can (7¼ ounces drained) large ripe olives
2 bunches radishes

**Each serving:** About 90 calories, 3 g protein, 16 g carbohydrate, 4 g total fat (0 g saturated), 0 mg cholesterol, 240 mg sodium.

1. *Blanch vegetables* (except celery): In 4-quart saucepan, heat *2 inches water* to boiling over high heat. Add carrots; heat to boiling. Cook 1 to 2 minutes, until tender-crisp. With slotted spoon, transfer carrots to bowl of cold water to stop cooking; drain well. Repeat with green beans and cauliflower.

2. *Prepare marinade:* In 1-cup glass measuring cup, mix ¾ cup vinegar, 4 teaspoons sugar, ½ teaspoon salt, and ¼ cup water. Pour marinade into large zip-tight plastic bag. (Repeat for each vegetable, following instructions below for flavoring.)

3. Place each vegetable in its marinade. Close bag and refrigerate up to 2 days, turning occasionally.

4. To serve, drain marinade from each vegetable. Arrange all pickled vegetables on tray or platter with olives and radishes.

*Lemon-Tarragon Celery:* Prepare basic marinade as in step 2, but add 1 teaspoon dried tarragon and strips of peel from 1 lemon. Marinate and serve as in steps 3 and 4.

*Peppercorn-Dill Carrots:* Blanch and cool carrots as in step 1. Prepare basic marinade as in step 2, but add ¼ cup chopped fresh dill (or 2 teaspoons dried dillweed) and 1 teaspoon whole black peppercorns. Marinate and serve as in steps 3 and 4.

*Spiced Cauliflower:* Blanch and cool cauliflower as in step 1. Prepare basic marinade as in step 2, but add 1 tablespoon pickling spice. Marinate and serve as in steps 3 and 4.

*Orange-Fennel Green Beans:* Blanch and cool beans as in step 1. Prepare basic marinade as in step 2, but add 1 teaspoon fennel seeds, crushed, and strips of peel from 1 small orange. Marinate and serve as in steps 3 and 4.

# Mexican Shrimp Skewers

**Prep:** 45 minutes    ◆    **Cook:** 3 minutes
**Makes** 20 appetizers

1. In 4-quart saucepan, heat *8 cups water* to boiling over high heat. Add shrimp and heat to boiling; cook 1 to 2 minutes, until shrimp turn opaque. Drain.
2. In large bowl, combine chiles, lime juice, cilantro, oil, sugar, salt, and pepper. Add shrimp and stir to coat thoroughly with dressing. If not serving kabobs right away, cover and refrigerate shrimp mixture.
3. Just before serving, cut each avocado in half lengthwise. With sharp knife, remove pit. Peel and cut avocados into 1¼-inch chunks. Gently stir avocado into shrimp mixture until thoroughly coated with chile dressing, being careful not to bruise avocado.
4. On each skewer, thread 2 shrimp and 2 chunks of avocado. Arrange skewers on large platter; garnish with lime and lemon wedges. Serve immediately.

▼ *M*EXICAN SHRIMP SKEWERS
◆

40 large shrimp (1¾ pounds), shelled and deveined
1 can (4 to 4½ ounces) mild green chiles, chopped, with their juice
2 tablespoons fresh lime juice
1 tablespoon chopped fresh cilantro or 1 teaspoon dried cilantro
1 tablespoon olive or vegetable oil
½ teaspoon sugar
¾ teaspoon salt
½ teaspoon ground black pepper
2 medium avocados
20 (12-inch) bamboo skewers
lime and lemon wedges for garnish

**Each appetizer:** About 49 calories, 3 g protein, 1 g carbohydrate, 4 g total fat (1 g saturated), 22 mg cholesterol, 127 mg sodium.

## Christmas Quesadillas

**Prep:** 40 minutes   ◆   **Bake:** 8 minutes
**Makes** 48 wedges

1 tablespoon vegetable oil
1 large onion, finely chopped
1 green pepper, finely chopped
1 red pepper, finely chopped
1 garlic clove, finely chopped
¼ teaspoon ground cumin
¼ teaspoon salt
2 tablespoons chopped fresh
   cilantro
12 (6- to 7-inch) flour tortillas
6 ounces Monterey Jack cheese
   with jalapeño chiles, shredded
   (1½ cups)
cilantro leaves and 1 hot red
   pepper for garnish

**Each wedge:** About 50 calories,
2 g protein, 6 g carbohydrate,
2 g total fat (1 g saturated),
4 mg cholesterol, 75 mg sodium.

1. In nonstick 10-inch skillet, heat oil over medium heat. Add onion and peppers; cook, stirring often, 15 minutes, or until golden and tender. Add garlic, cumin, and salt and cook, stirring often, 5 minutes longer. Remove skillet from heat; stir in cilantro.

2. Place 6 tortillas on work surface. Spread pepper mixture on tortillas; sprinkle with cheese. Top with remaining tortillas to make 6 quesadillas. If not serving right away, cover and refrigerate assembled quesadillas up to 6 hours.

3. To serve, preheat oven to 450°F. Place quesadillas on 2 large cookie sheets and bake 4 minutes per side, or until lightly browned. Transfer quesadillas to cutting board. Cut each into 8 wedges; top each wedge with a cilantro leaf for garnish. Garnish platter with a hot red pepper. Serve immediately.

# Pimiento-Studded Deviled Eggs

**Prep:** 40 minutes

**Makes** 24 appetizers

1. Slice each egg lengthwise in half. Gently remove yolks and place in small bowl; with fork, thoroughly mash yolks. Add pimientos, mayonnaise dressing, mustard, ground red pepper, and salt and stir until well mixed.
2. Place egg-white halves in 15½" by 10½" jelly-roll pan lined with paper towels (to prevent eggs from rolling). Spoon yolk mixture into egg-white halves. Cover and refrigerate until ready to serve.

12 large eggs, hard-cooked and shelled
¼ cup sliced pimientos, chopped
¼ cup low-fat mayonnaise dressing
1 tablespoon plus 1 teaspoon Dijon mustard
½ teaspoon ground red pepper (cayenne)
¼ teaspoon salt
fresh herb sprigs for garnish

**Each appetizer:** About 45 calories, 3 g protein, 1 g carbohydrate, 3 g total fat (1 g saturated), 107 mg cholesterol, 100 mg sodium.

◀ $\mathcal{P}$IMIENTO-STUDDED DEVILED EGGS AND SMOKED TROUT PÂTÉ

◆

# Smoked Trout Pâté

3 whole smoked trout
(1¼ pounds)
1 package (8 ounces) whipped
cream cheese
¼ cup low-fat mayonnaise
dressing
3 tablespoons lemon juice
⅛ teaspoon ground black pepper
1 tablespoon finely chopped
chives or green onion chives
for garnish
assorted crackers and cucumber
slices

**Each tablespoon pâté without crackers or cucumbers:** About 35 calories, 2 g protein, 1 g carbohydrate, 3 g total fat 1 g saturated), 7 mg cholesterol, 100 mg sodium.

**Prep:** 30 minutes
**Makes** about 3 cups

1. Cut head and tail from each trout; remove skin and bones and discard. In food processor with knife blade attached, puree trout, cream cheese, mayonnaise dressing, lemon juice, and black pepper until smooth.
2. Spoon trout mixture into medium bowl; stir in finely chopped chives. Cover and refrigerate if not serving right away.
3. To serve, allow refrigerated pâté to stand at room temperature 15 minutes to soften. Garnish with chives. Serve with crackers and cucumber slices.

# Sesame Pita Toasts

½ cup sesame seeds, toasted
2 tablespoons chopped fresh
parsley
2 teaspoons dried thyme
2 teaspoons grated lemon peel
½ teaspoon salt
¼ teaspoon coarsely ground
black pepper
1 package (7 ounces) 2-inch
mini pitas
2 tablespoons extravirgin olive oil

**Each toast:** About 50 calories, 1 g protein, 5 g carbohydrate, 3 g total fat (0 g saturated), 0 mg cholesterol, 75 mg sodium.

**Prep:** 25 minutes   ◆   **Bake:** 8 minutes
**Makes** 24 toasts

1. *Prepare spice mixture:* In blender, blend sesame seeds, parsley, thyme, lemon peel, salt, and pepper, stopping blender occasionally and scraping down sides with rubber spatula, until seeds are ground. Transfer spice mixture to medium bowl.
2. Brush tops of pitas with oil. Sprinkle oiled side of each pita with about 1½ teaspoons spice mixture; gently press spices onto pita. Place pitas on large cookie sheet. If not serving right away, cover and refrigerate up to 6 hours.
3. To serve, preheat oven to 450°F. Bake 8 minutes, or until pitas are crisp and golden.

# Caviar Pie

**Prep:** 25 minutes  ◆  **Cook:** 15 minutes plus standing
**Makes** about 3 cups

1. In 3-quart saucepan, combine eggs and enough *cold water* to cover eggs by at least 1 inch; heat to boiling over high heat. Remove saucepan from heat and cover; let stand 15 minutes. Pour off hot water and run cold water over eggs to cool. Remove shells.
2. In bowl, with pastry blender or fork, mash eggs. Stir in mayonnaise, dill, salt, pepper, and 2 tablespoons sour cream. Spoon mixture into 9-inch pie plate. Cover and refrigerate overnight or until ready to serve.
3. To serve, spread remaining sour cream evenly over egg mixture; top with caviar.

8 large eggs
⅓ cup mayonnaise
¼ cup chopped fresh dill or parsley
¼ teaspoon salt
¼ teaspoon ground black pepper
1 container (8 ounces) sour cream
1 jar (2 ounces) red lumpfish caviar

**Each tablespoon:**
About 35 calories, 2 g protein, 0 g carbohydrate, 3 g total fat (1 g saturated), 45 mg cholesterol, 50 mg sodium.

# Lacy Parmesan Crisps

**Prep:** 20 minutes  ◆  **Bake:** 6 to 7 minutes per batch
**Makes** about 2 dozen crisps

1. Preheat oven to 375°F. Line large cookie sheet with reusable nonstick bakeware liner. Spoon cheese by level measuring tablespoons, about 3 inches apart, onto cookie sheet. Spread each spoonful into 2-inch round.
2. Bake cheese rounds 6 to 7 minutes, until edges just begin to color. Transfer bakeware liner to wire rack; cool 2 minutes. Transfer crisps to paper towels. Repeat with remaining cheese. Store in airtight container up to 4 days.

6 ounces Parmesan cheese, coarsely shredded (1½ cups)

**Each crisp:** About 30 calories, 3 g protein, 0 g carbohydrate, 2 g total fat (1 g saturated), 6 mg cholesterol, 130 mg sodium.

▶ *L*ACY PARMESAN CRISPS

◆

# Roasted Red Pepper and Walnut Dip

4 medium red peppers
½ cup walnuts
½ teaspoon ground cumin
2 slices firm white bread, torn
   into pieces
2 tablespoons raspberry vinegar
1 tablespoon olive oil
½ teaspoon salt
⅛ teaspoon ground red pepper
   (cayenne)
toasted pita triangles

Each tablespoon: About
25 calories, 0 g protein,
2 g carbohydrate, 2 g total fat
(0 g saturated), 0 mg cholesterol,
40 mg sodium.

**Prep:** 30 minutes plus cooling    ♦    **Broil:** 10 minutes
**Makes** about 2 cups dip

1. Preheat broiler; line broiling pan with foil. Broil peppers at closest position to heat source, turning occasionally, 10 minutes, or until charred all over. Remove from broiler. Wrap peppers loosely in foil and allow to steam at room temperature 15 minutes, or until cool enough to handle.

2. Turn oven control to 350°F. Spread walnuts in 9" by 9" metal baking pan and bake 8 to 10 minutes, until toasted. In 1-quart saucepan, toast cumin over low heat 1 to 2 minutes, until very fragrant.

3. Remove peppers from foil; peel off skin; discard skin and seeds. Cut peppers into large pieces. In food processor with knife blade attached, process walnuts until ground. Add roasted peppers, cumin, bread, raspberry vinegar, oil, salt, and ground red pepper; puree until smooth. Transfer to bowl. Cover and refrigerate if not serving right away. Remove from refrigerator 30 minutes before serving. Serve with toasted pita triangles.

# Omelet Española Squares

2 tablespoons olive oil
2 large all-purpose potatoes
   (1 pound), chopped
1 medium onion, sliced
1 medium green pepper,
   finely chopped
¾ teaspoon salt
8 large eggs
¼ teaspoon coarsely ground black
   pepper
½ cup water
1 can (14½ ounces) diced
   tomatoes, drained
½ cup chopped pimiento-stuffed
   olives (salad olives)
fresh chives for garnish (optional)

Each square: About 25 calories,
1 g protein, 2 g carbohydrate,
1 g total fat (0 g saturated), 28 mg
cholesterol, 100 mg sodium.

**Prep:** 45 minutes    ♦    **Bake:** 15 to 20 minutes
**Makes** about 60 squares

1. In nonstick 10-inch skillet with oven-safe handle (or wrap handle with heavy-duty foil for baking in oven later), heat oil over medium heat. Add potatoes, onion, green pepper, and ¼ teaspoon salt and cook, stirring occasionally, about 20 minutes, until vegetables are tender.

2. Meanwhile, preheat oven to 400°F. In medium bowl, with wire whisk or fork, beat eggs with pepper, remaining ½ teaspoon salt, and water. Stir in tomatoes and olives. Stir egg mixture into potato mixture in skillet; cover and cook 5 minutes, or until egg mixture begins to set around edge. Remove cover and place skillet in oven; bake 15 to 20 minutes, until omelet is set.

3. Carefully invert omelet onto large flat plate. Let cool before cutting into 1-inch squares. Garnish with chives if you like.

# Soups

# Green Gumbo

**Prep:** 20 minutes ◆ **Cook:** 40 minutes
**Makes** 10 cups or 8 first-course servings

1. In 5-quart Dutch oven, cook bacon over medium-low heat until browned. With slotted spoon, transfer bacon to paper towels to drain. Reserve for garnish.
2. Discard all but 2 tablespoons drippings from Dutch oven. Stir in flour, salt, and ground red pepper and cook over medium heat, stirring frequently, about 5 minutes, until golden brown.
3. Stir in broth, fresh greens, spinach, potato, and water; heat to boiling over high heat. Reduce heat; cover and simmer, stirring occasionally, 20 to 24 minutes, until soup thickens slightly and greens are tender. To serve, sprinkle bacon over soup.

8 slices bacon, cut into ½-inch pieces
¼ cup all-purpose flour
1 teaspoon salt
¼ teaspoon ground red pepper (cayenne)
2 cans (14½ ounces each) chicken broth
1½ pounds fresh greens (collard or mustard, or a combination), coarse stems removed and leaves cut into ½-inch pieces
1 package (10 ounces) frozen chopped spinach, thawed and squeezed dry
1 large all-purpose potato (8 ounces), peeled and grated
4 cups water

**Each serving:** About 145 calories, 7 g protein, 14 g carbohydrate, 7 g total fat (3 g saturated), 9 mg cholesterol, 735 mg sodium.

# Cauliflower-Cheddar Soup

**Prep:** 35 minutes ◆ **Cook:** 25 minutes
**Makes** about 9 cups or 8 first-course servings

1. In 4-quart saucepan, melt butter over medium heat. Add onion and cook, stirring occasionally, about 10 minutes, until golden. Stir in flour and salt; cook, stirring frequently, 2 minutes. Gradually stir in milk, broth, and water. Add cauliflower and heat to boiling over high heat. Reduce heat; cover and simmer about 10 minutes, until cauliflower is tender.
2. In blender, with center part of blender cover removed to allow steam to escape, puree cauliflower mixture in small batches until smooth. Pour pureed mixture into large bowl after each batch.
3. Return mixture to saucepan; heat soup, stirring occasionally, until hot. Remove saucepan from heat; stir in mustard and 1½ cups cheese until melted and smooth. Garnish soup with remaining cheese to serve.

2 tablespoons butter or margarine
1 medium onion, chopped
¼ cup all-purpose flour
½ teaspoon salt
2 cups milk
1 can (14½ ounces) chicken broth
1½ cups water
1 head cauliflower (2½ pounds), cut into 1-inch pieces
1 teaspoon Dijon mustard
1 package (8 ounces) shredded sharp Cheddar cheese (2 cups)

**Each serving:** About 230 calories, 14 g carbohydrates, 13 g protein, 15 g total fat (8 g saturated), 41 mg cholesterol, 575 mg sodium.

# Butternut Soup

**Prep:** 45 minutes ◆ **Cook:** 20 minutes
**Makes** about 8¾ cups or 12 first-course servings

1. Prepare Cinnamon Croutons.
2. Cut off root end from leek. Cut leek lengthwise in half; rinse with cold running water to remove sand. Coarsely chop white and pale-green part of leek; discard tough dark-green part.
3. In 5-quart Dutch oven or saucepot, melt butter over medium-high heat. Add carrots, onion, and leek and cook, stirring occasionally, about 10 minutes, until browned. Add squash, broth, salt, and water; heat to boiling. Reduce heat; cover and simmer 15 to 20 minutes, until squash is very tender.
4. In blender, with center part of cover removed to allow steam to escape, puree squash mixture in small batches until smooth. Pour pureed soup into large bowl after each batch.
5. Return soup to Dutch oven; stir in half-and-half. Heat soup, stirring occasionally, until hot. Serve with Cinnamon Croutons.

Cinnamon Croutons (see following page)
1 medium leek
3 tablespoons butter or margarine
2 medium carrots, peeled and coarsely chopped
1 medium onion, coarsely chopped
1 medium butternut squash (2½ pounds), peeled and cut into 1-inch pieces
1 can (14½ ounces) chicken broth
½ teaspoon salt
2¼ cups water
½ cup half-and-half or light cream

**Each serving of soup with croutons:** About 150 calories, 3 g protein, 20 g carbohydrate, 7 g total fat (2 g saturated), 5 mg cholesterol, 355 mg sodium.

◀ *G*REEN GUMBO, BUTTERNUT SOUP, AND CAULIFLOWER-CHEDDAR SOUP *(clockwise from top left)*

◆

*Cinnamon Croutons:* Preheat oven to 400°F. Cut ½ loaf (4 ounces) French bread into ¾-inch cubes (about 4 cups). In bowl, combine 3 tablespoons melted butter or margarine, ¼ teaspoon ground cinnamon, scant ⅛ teaspoon salt, and bread cubes; toss to coat. Spread bread cubes in 15½" by 10½" jelly-roll pan; bake 10 to 12 minutes, until golden.

# Mushroom and Wild Rice Soup

**Prep:** 45 minutes ◆ **Cook:** 1 hour
**Makes** about 9 cups or 8 first-course servings

½ cup wild rice
2½ cups plus 2 tablespoons water
1 package (½ ounce) dried
  mushrooms
2 cups boiling water
2 tablespoons olive oil
2 celery stalks, chopped
1 large onion, chopped
1 package (10 ounces)
  mushrooms, cut into ¼-inch-
  thick slices
2 cans (14½ ounces each)
  chicken broth
1 tablespoon soy sauce
½ teaspoon dried thyme
¼ teaspoon coarsely ground
  black pepper
¼ cup cream sherry

**Each serving:** About 130 calories, 5 g protein, 16 g carbohydrate, 4 g total fat (1 g saturated), 4 mg cholesterol, 430 mg sodium.

1. In 3-quart saucepan, heat wild rice and 2½ cups water to boiling over high heat. Reduce heat; cover and simmer 45 minutes, or until rice is tender and most of water has been absorbed.
2. Meanwhile, in 4-cup glass measuring cup, add dried mushrooms to 2 cups boiling water; set aside.
3. In nonstick 12-inch skillet, heat 1 tablespoon oil over medium heat. Add celery, onion, and 2 tablespoons water; cook about 10 minutes, until vegetables are tender and lightly browned. Transfer mixture to 4-quart saucepan.
4. In same skillet, heat remaining 1 tablespoon oil over medium-high heat. Add sliced mushrooms; cook about 10 minutes, until mushrooms are tender and lightly browned. Transfer to 4-quart saucepan with celery mixture.
5. With slotted spoon, remove dried mushrooms from soaking liquid and coarsely chop; strain liquid. Add dried mushrooms and their liquid to saucepan; stir in broth, soy sauce, thyme, pepper, and wild rice with any cooking liquid; heat to boiling over high heat. Stir in sherry. Reduce heat; cover and simmer 5 minutes.

# Chicken and Escarole Soup with Meatballs

**Prep:** 1 hour  ◆  **Cook:** 1 hour 15 minutes
**Makes** about 16 cups or 14 first-course servings

1. In 8-quart Dutch oven or saucepot, combine chicken, onion, peppercorns, bay leaf, and water; heat to boiling over high heat. Reduce heat; cover and simmer 1 hour 15 minutes, or until chicken is tender.

2. *Meanwhile, prepare meatballs:* In large bowl, with hands, combine ground meat, garlic, egg, parsley, pepper, ½ cup Romano cheese, and ¾ teaspoon salt. In small bowl with fork, mix bread crumbs and milk to form a thick paste. Mix bread-crumb mixture into meat mixture just until blended. Shape meat mixture into about seventy 1-inch meatballs (for easier shaping, use slightly wet hands) and place on cookie sheet; cover and refrigerate 30 minutes.

3. Transfer chicken to bowl; set aside until cool enough to handle. Discard skin and bones; cut chicken into bite-size pieces. Reserve 2 cups cut-up chicken; refrigerate remaining chicken for another use. Pour chicken broth through sieve lined with paper towels into large bowl. Let stand until fat separates from meat juice. Skim fat from broth and discard.

4. Return broth to clean Dutch oven or saucepot. Add canned broth and remaining 2 teaspoons salt; heat to boiling over high heat. Stir in carrots and celery; heat to boiling. Reduce heat; cover and simmer 8 to 10 minutes, until vegetables are tender. Add meatballs and remaining ¼ cup Romano cheese; heat to boiling over high heat. Reduce heat; cover and simmer 15 minutes, or until meatballs are cooked through. Stir in escarole and reserved chicken; heat through. Serve with grated Romano cheese to sprinkle over each serving.

1 chicken (4 pounds), cut up
1 large onion, cut in half
¼ teaspoon whole black peppercorns
1 bay leaf
12 cups water
1 pound ground meat for meatloaf (a mixture of ground beef, pork, and veal)
2 garlic cloves, crushed with garlic press
1 large egg, beaten
¼ cup chopped fresh flat-leaf parsley
½ teaspoon ground black pepper
¾ cup grated Romano cheese, plus additional for serving
2¾ teaspoons salt
1 cup plain dried bread crumbs
⅓ cup milk
1 can (14½ ounces) chicken broth
3 medium carrots, peeled and sliced
2 medium celery stalks, sliced
1 small head escarole (8 ounces), cut into ½-inch strips, with tough stems discarded

**Each serving:** About 235 calories, 18 g protein, 10 g carbohydrate, 13 g total fat (5 g saturated), 61 mg cholesterol, 760 mg sodium.

# Entrees

▲ PORK CROWN
ROAST WITH APPLE
STUFFING P.31

## Roast Turkey with Pan Gravy

1 fresh or frozen (thawed) turkey
  (14 pounds)
2 teaspoons salt
½ teaspoon coarsely ground
  black pepper
2 tablespoons all-purpose flour
fresh herbs and grapes for garnish

**Each serving turkey without
skin or gravy:** About
330 calories, 57 g protein,
0 g carbohydrate, 10 g total fat
(3 g saturated), 149 mg
cholesterol, 250 mg sodium.

**Each ¼ cup of gravy:** About
65 calories, 7 g protein,
2 g carbohydrate, 4 g total fat
(1 g saturated) 63 mg cholesterol,
110 mg sodium.

*R*OAST TURKEY ▶
WITH PAN GRAVY
◆

**Prep:** 45 minutes   ◆   **Roast:** about 3 hours 45 minutes
**Makes** 14 main-dish servings

1. Preheat oven to 325°F. Remove giblets and neck from turkey; reserve for making pan gravy. Rinse turkey with cold running water and drain well.
2. Fasten neck skin to back with 1 or 2 skewers. With turkey breast side up, fold wings under back of turkey so they stay in place. Depending on brand of turkey, with string, tie legs and tail together, or push drumsticks under band of skin, or use stuffing clamp.
3. Place turkey, breast side up, on rack in large roasting pan (17" by 11½"). Rub turkey all over with 1½ teaspoons salt and pepper. Cover turkey with a loose tent of foil. Roast about 3 hours 45 minutes; start checking for doneness during last hour of roasting.
4. While turkey is roasting, in 3-quart saucepan, combine gizzard, heart, neck, and enough water to cover and heat to boiling over high heat. Reduce heat; cover and simmer 45 minutes. Add liver and cook 15 minutes longer. Drain, reserving broth. Pull meat from neck; discard bones. Coarsely chop neck meat and giblets. Cover and refrigerate meat and broth separately.
5. To brown turkey, remove foil during last 1 hour of roasting time and baste occasionally with pan drippings. Turkey is done when temperature on meat thermometer inserted in thickest part of thigh next to body registers 180° to 185°F and drumstick feels soft when pressed with fingers protected by paper towels. (Breast temperature should be 170° to 175°F.)

6. When turkey is done, place on warm large platter; keep warm. Prepare pan gravy: Remove rack from roasting pan. Pour pan drippings through sieve into 4-cup measure or medium bowl. Add 1 cup giblet broth to roasting pan and stir until brown bits are loosened; pour into drippings in measuring cup. Let stand until fat separates from meat juice. Spoon 2 tablespoons fat from drippings into 2-quart saucepan; skim and discard any remaining fat. Add remaining giblet broth and enough water to meat juice in cup to equal 3 cups.

7. Into fat in saucepan, stir flour and remaining ½ teaspoon salt; cook, over medium heat, stirring, until flour turns golden brown. Gradually stir in meat-juice mixture and cook, stirring, until gravy boils and thickens slightly. Stir in reserved giblets and neck meat; heat through. Pour gravy into gravy boat. Makes 3 cups.

8. To serve, garnish with fresh herbs and grapes. Serve with gravy. Remove skin from turkey before eating, if you like.

CRISPY ▶
CITRUS GOOSE
◆

# Crispy Citrus Goose

**Prep:** 30 minutes  ◆  **Roast:** about 4 hours 30 minutes
**Makes** 10 main-dish servings

1. Preheat oven to 400°F. Remove giblets and neck from goose; refrigerate or freeze for another use. Discard fat from body cavity and any excess skin. Rinse goose with cold running water and drain well.

2. With breast side up, fold wings under back so they stay in place. Place thyme sprigs, bay leaves, and 6 orange halves in body cavity. With string, tie legs and tail together. Fold neck skin over back.

3. Place goose, breast side up, on rack in large roasting pan (17" by 11½"). With fork, prick skin in many places. In cup, mix pepper, dried thyme, and 1 teaspoon salt; rub mixture over goose.

4. Cover roasting pan with foil and roast goose 1 hour 30 minutes. Turn oven control to 325°F, and roast goose 2 hours longer.

5. Meanwhile, from remaining 4 orange halves squeeze ¾ cup juice. Stir in cornstarch, 1 tablespoon orange-flavored liqueur, and remaining ¼ teaspoon salt; set aside. In cup, mix orange marmalade with remaining 2 tablespoons orange-flavored liqueur.

6. Remove foil and roast goose 45 minutes longer. Remove goose from oven and turn oven control to 450°F. With spoon or bulb baster, remove as much fat as possible from pan into 8-cup glass measure or large bowl. Brush orange-marmalade mixture over goose. Roast goose 10 minutes longer, or until skin is golden and crisp. Goose is done when temperature on meat thermometer inserted into thickest part of meat between breast and thigh, registers 180° to 185°F and juices run clear when thickest part of thigh is pierced with tip of knife.

7. Transfer goose to warm large platter; let stand 10 minutes to set juices for easier slicing.

8. *Prepare sauce:* Remove rack from roasting pan. Pour remaining pan drippings through sieve into 8-cup glass measure. Let stand until fat separates from meat juice; pour off and discard fat (there should be about 5 cups fat and 1 cup meat juice; if necessary, add enough *water* to meat juice to equal 1 cup). Return meat juice to pan and add reserved orange-juice mixture. Heat sauce mixture to boiling over medium heat; boil 30 seconds.

9. To serve, garnish platter with orange wedges and thyme sprigs. Pour orange sauce into gravy boat.

1 fresh or frozen (thawed) goose (12 pounds)
1 bunch fresh thyme
4 bay leaves
5 medium oranges, each cut in half
½ teaspoon coarsely ground black pepper
½ teaspoon dried thyme
1¼ teaspoons salt
2 tablespoons cornstarch
3 tablespoons orange-flavored liqueur
½ cup orange marmalade
orange wedges and thyme sprigs for garnish

**Each serving of goose without skin:** About 460 calories, 50 g protein, 12 g carbohydrate, 25 g total fat (8 g saturated), 170 mg cholesterol, 345 mg sodium.

**Each tablespoon sauce:** About 5 calories, 0 g protein, 1 g carbohydrate, 0 g total fat (0 g saturated), 0 mg cholesterol, 20 mg sodium.

▲ **A**PPLE-GINGER
**GLAZED HAM**

◆

# Apple-Ginger Glazed Ham

**Prep:** 15 minutes ◆ **Cook:** 3 to 3 hours 30 minutes
**Makes** 20 main-dish servings

**1 fully cooked smoked whole ham
  (14 pounds)
½ cup apple jelly
¼ teaspoon ground ginger
fresh herbs for garnish**

**Each serving:** About 175 calories,
30 g protein, 10 g carbohydrate,
5 g total fat (2 g saturated), 81 mg
cholesterol, 1,500 mg sodium.

1. Preheat oven to 325°F. Remove skin and trim some fat from ham, leaving about ¼-inch fat covering.
2. Place ham on rack in large roasting pan (17" by 11½"). Bake ham 2 hours 30 minutes.
3. *After ham has baked 2 hours 30 minutes, prepare glaze:* In small saucepan, combine apple jelly and ginger and heat to boiling over medium-high heat; boil 2 minutes. Brush ham with some glaze. Bake ham 30 minutes to 1 hour longer, brushing occasionally with remaining glaze, until meat thermometer inserted into center of ham registers 140°F (15 to 18 minutes per pound total cooking time).
4. When ham is done, transfer to warm large platter; let stand 20 minutes to set juices for easier slicing. Garnish with herbs.

# Pork Crown Roast with Apple Stuffing

**Prep:** 30 minutes    ◆    **Roast:** about 2 hours
**Makes** 14 main-dish servings

1. Preheat oven to 325°F. Rub inside and outside of pork roast with 1 teaspoon salt and ¼ teaspoon pepper. Place pork, rib ends down, in large roasting pan (17" by 11½"). Roast pork 1 hour.
2. Meanwhile, in 5-quart Dutch oven, melt butter over medium heat. Add celery and onion and cook, stirring often, about 10 minutes, until tender. Add apples and cook 6 to 8 minutes longer, until tender. Remove from heat; stir in bread pieces, apple juice, poultry seasoning, egg, 1 teaspoon salt, and ¼ teaspoon pepper.
3. When pork has roasted 1 hour, remove from oven and turn rib ends up. Spoon about 4 cups stuffing into cavity. (Place remaining stuffing in greased 1½-quart casserole; bake, uncovered, during last 30 minutes of pork roasting time.)
4. Return pork to oven and continue roasting about 1 hour longer, until meat thermometer inserted between 2 ribs into thickest part of meat

1 pork rib crown roast
   (7 pounds), well trimmed
2¼ teaspoons salt
½ plus ⅛ teaspoon ground
   black pepper
6 tablespoons butter or margarine
4 medium celery stalks,
   finely chopped
1 large onion, finely chopped
3 large Golden Delicious apples
   (1½ pounds), peeled, cored,
   and finely chopped
12 slices firm white bread,
   cut into ½-inch pieces
   (about 8 cups)
½ cup apple juice
1 teaspoon poultry seasoning
1 large egg
¼ cup applejack brandy,
   Calvados, or apple juice
3 tablespoons all-purpose flour
1 can (14½ ounces) chicken broth
kale and small apples for garnish

**Each serving pork with stuffing:** About 480 calories, 35 g protein, 18 g carbohydrate, 30 g total fat (10 g saturated), 95 mg cholesterol, 565 mg sodium.

**Each tablespoon gravy:** About 15 calories, 0 g protein, 1 g carbohydrate, 1 g total fat (0 g saturated), 1 mg cholesterol, 50 mg sodium.

◀ *P*ORK CROWN ROAST
   WITH APPLE STUFFING

◆

registers 155°F. Internal temperature of meat will rise to 160°F upon standing. If stuffing browns too quickly during roasting, cover it loosely with foil.

5. When roast is done, transfer to warm large platter; let stand 15 minutes to set juices for easier slicing.

6. *Meanwhile, prepare gravy:* Pour pan drippings into 2-cup measuring cup or medium bowl; set pan aside. Let stand until fat separates from meat juice. Spoon 3 tablespoons fat from drippings (add enough melted butter, if necessary, to equal 3 tablespoons) into 2-quart saucepan; skim and discard any remaining fat. Add applejack to roasting pan and stir until brown bits are loosened; add to meat juice in cup.

7. Into drippings in saucepan, stir flour, remaining ¼ teaspoon salt and ⅛ teaspoon pepper; cook over medium heat, stirring, 1 minute. Gradually stir in meat-juice mixture and broth and cook, stirring, until gravy boils and thickens. Makes about 2½ cups.

8. To serve, garnish with kale and apples. Serve pork with gravy and stuffing.

# Beef Rib Roast
# with Creamy Horseradish Sauce

**Prep:** 15 minutes    ♦    **Roast:** 3 hours
**Makes** 10 main-dish servings

1. Preheat oven to 325°F. In medium roasting pan (14" by 10"), place beef roast, fat side up. In mortar with pestle, crush peppercorns with salt. Rub peppercorn mixture over roast.

2. Roast beef until meat thermometer inserted into center registers 140°F (about 20 minutes per pound). Internal temperature will rise to 145°F (medium) upon standing. Or, roast to desired doneness.

3. When beef is done, transfer to warm large platter and let stand 15 minutes to set juices for easier slicing. Meanwhile, prepare Creamy Horseradish Sauce.

*Creamy Horseradish Sauce:* In small bowl, mix 1 jar (6 ounces) prepared white horseradish, drained, ½ cup mayonnaise, 1 teaspoon sugar, and ½ teaspoon salt. Whip ½ cup heavy or whipping cream; fold into horseradish mixture. Makes about 1⅔ cups.

◄ *B*EEF RIB ROAST
WITH CREAMY
HORSERADISH SAUCE

♦

1 (3-rib) beef rib roast, small end (about 7 pounds), chine bone removed
3 tablespoons whole tricolor peppercorns (red, green, and black)
1 teaspoon salt
Creamy Horseradish Sauce (see below)

**Each serving beef:** About 410 calories, 35 g protein, 1 g carbohydrate, 29 g total fat (12 g saturated), 97 mg cholesterol, 295 mg sodium

**Each tablespoon sauce:** About 50 calories, 0 g protein, 1 g carbohydrate, 5 g total fat (2 g saturated), 8 mg cholesterol, 70 mg sodium.

# Tarragon-Roasted Salmon with Caper Sauce

**Prep:** 20 minutes    ◆    **Roast:** about 40 minutes
**Makes** 10 main-dish servings

## Caper Sauce

¾ cup sour cream
½ cup mayonnaise
¼ cup milk
3 tablespoons capers, drained
   and chopped
2 tablespoons chopped fresh
   tarragon
½ teaspoon grated lemon peel
⅛ teaspoon ground black pepper

## Salmon

2 large lemons, thinly sliced
1 whole salmon (5½ pounds),
   cleaned and scaled, with
   head and tail removed
2 tablespoons olive oil
½ teaspoon salt
½ teaspoon coarsely ground
   black pepper
1 large bunch fresh tarragon
1 small bunch fresh flat-leaf
   parsley
lemon wedges and tarragon
   sprigs for garnish

**Each serving fish without
sauce:** About 180 calories,
25 g protein, 0 g carbohydrate,
8 g total fat (2 g saturated),
45 mg cholesterol, 160 mg
sodium.

**Each tablespoon sauce:**
About 60 calories, 0 g protein,
1 g carbohydrate, 6 g total fat
(2 g saturated), 6 mg cholesterol,
80 mg sodium.

1. *Prepare caper sauce:* In medium bowl, with fork, mix all sauce ingredients until blended. Cover and refrigerate up to 2 days or until ready to serve. Makes about 1⅓ cups.
2. *Prepare salmon:* Preheat oven to 450°F. Line 15½" by 10½" jelly-roll pan with foil.
3. Place one-third of lemon slices in a row down center of pan. Rub outside of salmon with oil. Place salmon on top of lemon slices. Sprinkle cavity with salt and pepper. Place tarragon and parsley sprigs inside cavity along with half of remaining lemon slices. Place remaining lemon slices on top of fish.
4. Roast salmon about 40 minutes, until fish turns opaque throughout and flakes easily when tested with a fork. Remove lemon slices and skin from top of salmon; discard. Transfer salmon to warm large platter. Garnish with lemon wedges and tarragon sprigs.  Serve with caper sauce.

*Tip:* To serve a whole fish as elegantly as any restaurant, peel off the top skin with a fork and knife. Slide the knife under the front section of fillet and, using a wide spatula, transfer the top fillet to a long platter. Slide the knife under the backbone and lift it away from the bottom fillet. Slide the knife between the bottom skin and fillet and transfer the fillet to the platter.

*TARRAGON-ROASTED SALMON* ▶
**WITH CAPER SAUCE**
◆

▲ CRANBERRY-PEAR RELISH
AND CRANBERRY-
ORANGE RELISH P. 51

# Side Dishes

## Green Beans with Honey-Pecan Butter

½ cup pecans
½ cup butter or margarine,
   softened
2 tablespoons honey
½ teaspoon coarsely ground
   black pepper
2 pounds green beans, trimmed

**Each serving:** About 75 calories,
2 g protein, 9 g carbohydrate,
4 g total fat (1 g saturated),
0 mg cholesterol, 40 mg sodium.

**Prep:** 30 minutes plus chilling or freezing   ◆   **Cook:** about 12 minutes
**Makes** 8 accompaniment servings

1. Preheat oven to 375°F. Place nuts in 8" by 8" metal baking pan. Bake 8 to 10 minutes, until lightly toasted. Cool completely. In food processor, with knife blade attached, process pecans until finely ground.
2. In bowl, with spoon, mix butter with honey, pepper, and ground pecans until blended. Spoon mixture into a 6-inch-long strip across width of sheet of plastic wrap or waxed paper. Freeze about 20 minutes, until slightly firm. Roll mixture, covered with plastic wrap or waxed paper, back and forth, to make a 6-inch-long log. Wrap well; refrigerate up to 2 days or freeze up to 2 months (thaw in refrigerator 1 hour before using).
3. In 12-inch skillet, heat *½ inch water* and green beans to boiling over high heat. Reduce heat; simmer 5 to 10 minutes, until beans are just tender-crisp. Drain; rinse with cold running water to stop cooking. Transfer beans to zip-tight plastic bag and refrigerate up to 2 days if not serving right away.
4. To serve, in 12-inch skillet, heat cooked beans with one-fourth of pecan butter over medium heat until butter melts and beans are hot.

𝒮PICY PEARL ONIONS ▶
AND
GREEN BEANS WITH
HONEY-PECAN BUTTER
◆

# Spicy Pearl Onions

**Prep:** 45 minutes  ◆  **Cook:** about 20 minutes
**Makes** 8 accompaniment servings

3 baskets (10 ounces each)
   pearl onions
3 tablespoons dark brown sugar
2 tablespoons butter or margarine
2 teaspoons raspberry vinegar
1 teaspoon tomato paste
¼ teaspoon salt
¼ teaspoon ground red pepper
   (cayenne) or 1 teaspoon
   chipotle chile puree

**Each serving:** About 85 calories,
1 g protein, 14 g carbohydrate,
3 g total fat (1 g saturated),
0 mg cholesterol, 120 mg sodium.

1. In deep 12-inch skillet, heat *1 inch water* to boiling over high heat. Add onions; heat to boiling. Reduce heat; cover and simmer 5 to 10 minutes, until onions are tender. Drain well. Wipe skillet dry.

2. Peel onions, leaving a little of the root ends to help hold their shape during glazing. Let onions cool slightly; cover and refrigerate up to 24 hours, if not serving right away.

3. To serve, in 12-inch skillet, combine brown sugar and remaining ingredients and heat over high heat, stirring often, until melted. Add onions and cook, stirring occasionally, about 10 minutes, until onions are browned and glazed.

# Braised Celery

**Prep:** 20 minutes  ◆  **Cook:** 45 to 55 minutes
**Makes** 6 accompaniment servings

1 bunch celery
1 tablespoon butter or margarine
2 slices bacon, finely chopped
1 small onion, finely chopped
1 small carrot, peeled and
   finely chopped
1 garlic clove, finely chopped
1 tablespoon tomato paste
½ cup chicken broth
½ cup water

**Each serving:** About 90 calories,
2 g protein, 7 g carbohydrate,
7 g total fat (2 g saturated),
5 mg cholesterol, 245 mg sodium.

1. Trim ends of celery stalks. With paring knife or vegetable peeler, remove tough strings from stalks. Cut stalks crosswise into thirds.

2. In 12-inch skillet, melt butter with bacon over medium heat. Stir in onion and carrot and cook 8 minutes, or until vegetables are tender. Stir in garlic and cook 30 seconds. Add tomato paste and cook, stirring, 1 minute longer. Stir in broth and water; heat to boiling. Stir in celery, spooning vegetable mixture over celery; heat to boiling. Reduce heat; cover and simmer 40 to 45 minutes, until celery is very tender and most of liquid has evaporated. Transfer to serving bowl, or cover and refrigerate up to 24 hours if not serving immediately.

3. To serve, return celery mixture to skillet and cook over medium heat about 10 minutes, until heated through.

# Green Beans with Toasted Benne Seeds

**Prep:** 25 minutes ◆ **Cook:** 20 minutes
**Makes** 20 accompaniment servings

1. *Prepare dressing:* In small bowl, with wire whisk or fork, mix lemon juice, mustard, and salt until blended. In thin, steady stream, gradually whisk in oil.
2. In 8-quart Dutch oven, heat *1 inch water* to boiling over high heat. Add half of green beans and heat to boiling. Reduce heat; cover and simmer 5 to 10 minutes, until beans are just tender-crisp. Transfer beans to colander; drain well. Repeat with remaining beans.
3. In large bowl, toss warm beans with dressing; cover and refrigerate until ready to serve. Toss beans with sesame seeds just before serving.

3 tablespoons lemon juice
1 tablespoon plus 1 teaspoon
   Dijon mustard
1 teaspoon salt
¼ cup olive oil
4 pounds green beans, trimmed
2 tablespoons sesame seeds
   (benne seeds), toasted

**Each serving:** About 60 calories, 2 g protein, 7 g carbohydrate, 3 g total fat (0 g saturated), 0 mg cholesterol, 135 mg sodium.

◀ *B*RAISED CELERY

◆

# Sautéed Cabbage with Peas

**Prep:** 10 minutes ◆ **Cook:** about 40 minutes
**Makes** 8 accompaniment servings

1. In 12-inch skillet, melt butter over medium heat. Add onion and cook, stirring often, about 8 minutes, until tender and golden.
2. Add cabbage, salt, sugar, and pepper and cook, stirring often, about 5 minutes, until cabbage is tender-crisp. Stir in broth and cook cabbage mixture 10 minutes longer, or until cabbage is tender. Spoon cabbage mixture into bowl; cover and refrigerate up to 24 hours, if not serving right away.
3. To serve, return cabbage mixture to skillet; add frozen peas and dill. Cook over medium heat, stirring frequently, 12 to 15 minutes, until heated through.

2 tablespoons butter or margarine
1 medium onion, thinly sliced
1 small head savoy cabbage
    (2 pounds), cored and cut
    into ½-inch-thick slices,
    with tough ribs discarded
¾ teaspoon salt
½ teaspoon sugar
¼ teaspoon coarsely ground
    black pepper
½ cup chicken broth
1 package (10 ounces) frozen
    baby peas
¼ cup chopped fresh dill

**Each serving:** About 90 calories,
4 g protein, 13 g carbohydrate,
3 g total fat (1 g saturated),
0 mg cholesterol, 345 mg sodium.

# Mashed Root Vegetables

**Prep:** 15 minutes ◆ **Cook:** 25 minutes ◆ **Bake:** about 30 minutes
**Makes** 8 accompaniment servings

1. In 5- or 6-quart saucepot, combine root vegetables, potatoes, 2 teaspoons salt, and enough *water* to cover; heat to boiling over high heat. Reduce heat to medium and cook 15 minutes, or until vegetables and potatoes are tender. Drain.
2. Return vegetables to saucepot; add butter, pepper, and ½ teaspoon salt and mash with potato masher until smooth. Spoon mixture into 1½-quart casserole; cool slightly.
3. To serve, preheat oven to 350°F. Cover casserole and bake 30 minutes, or until heated through. Sprinkle with nutmeg.

*Tip:* Menu planning is a talent to be nurtured. An inspiring choice of side dishes, mixed and matched with your entree, should provide variety in color, texture, and taste. Try some of the more unusual cabbages and root vegetables; they're ex-treme-ly rich in nutrients and delicious, too!

2 pounds assorted root vegetables
    (carrots, celery root (celeriac),
    parsnips, white turnips, and/or
    rutabaga), peeled and cut into
    1-inch pieces (5 cups)
1 pound all-purpose potatoes,
    peeled and cut into 1-inch
    pieces (2½ to 3 cups)
2½ teaspoons salt
3 tablespoons butter or margarine
¼ teaspoon ground black pepper
pinch nutmeg

**Each serving:** About 150 calories,
3 g protein, 26 g carbohydrate,
5 g total fat (1 g saturated),
0 mg cholesterol, 305 mg sodium.

◀ *S*AUTÉED CABBAGE WITH PEAS, AND
    MASHED ROOT VEGETABLES

# Apricot-Ginger Carrots

**Prep:** 10 minutes ◆ **Cook:** about 30 minutes
**Makes** 8 accompaniment servings

2 bags (16 ounces each) peeled
    baby carrots
2 tablespoons butter or margarine
2 green onions, finely chopped
1 large garlic clove, finely
    chopped
1 tablespoon minced, peeled
    fresh ginger
⅓ cup apricot jam
1 tablespoon balsamic vinegar
¼ teaspoon salt
pinch ground red pepper
    (cayenne)

**Each serving:** About 115 calories,
1 g protein, 22 g carbohydrate,
3 g total fat (1 g saturated),
0 mg cholesterol, 145 mg sodium.

1. Place steamer basket in deep 12-inch skillet with *1 inch water*; heat to boiling over high heat. Add carrots and reduce heat to medium; cover and cook 10 to 12 minutes, just until carrots are tender-crisp. Remove carrots and rinse with cold running water to stop cooking; drain well. Place carrots in large zip-tight plastic bag; refrigerate until ready to serve.

2. In 12-inch skillet, melt butter over medium heat. Add green onions, garlic, and ginger and cook, stirring often, about 3 minutes, until tender. Add apricot jam, vinegar, salt, and ground red pepper and cook, stirring often, 3 to 4 minutes longer. Let glaze cool slightly. Pour glaze into small container; cover and refrigerate until ready to serve.

3. To serve, in 12-inch skillet, cook glaze and carrots over medium-high heat 5 minutes. Increase heat to high and cook, stirring occasionally, 3 minutes, or until carrots are well coated and heated through.

# Brussels Sprouts with Bacon

**Prep:** 15 minutes ◆ **Cook:** 15 minutes
**Makes** 8 accompaniment servings

3 containers (10 ounces each)
    Brussels sprouts, trimmed
6 slices bacon
1 tablespoon olive oil
2 garlic cloves, crushed with
    garlic press
½ teaspoon salt
¼ teaspoon coarsely ground
    black pepper
¼ cup pine nuts (pignoli),
    toasted

**Each serving:** About 120 calories,
6 g protein, 10 g carbohydrate,
8 g total fat (2 g saturated),
6 mg cholesterol, 235 mg sodium.

1. In 4-quart saucepan, heat *1 inch water* to boiling over high heat. Add Brussels sprouts; heat to boiling. Reduce heat; cover and simmer 5 minutes, or until Brussels sprouts are tender-crisp. Drain. (If you like, Brussels sprouts can be cooked a day ahead. After draining, rinse with cold water to stop cooking; cover and refrigerate until ready to stir-fry in step 3.)

2. In nonstick 12-inch skillet, cook bacon over medium-low heat until browned. Transfer bacon to paper towels to drain; crumble.

3. Pour off all but 1 tablespoon drippings from skillet. Add oil and heat over medium-high heat. Add Brussels sprouts, garlic, salt, and pepper. Cook, stirring frequently, about 5 minutes, until Brussels sprouts are browned. Top with pine nuts and crumbled bacon.

# Wild Rice and Orzo Pilaf

**Prep:** 25 minutes ◆ **Cook:** 55 minutes ◆ **Bake:** 45 minutes
**Makes** about 9 cups or 12 accompaniment servings

1. Prepare orzo and wild rice, separately, as labels direct.
2. Meanwhile, in 12-inch skillet, melt butter over medium heat. Add onion and celery and cook, stirring occasionally, about 10 minutes, until tender. Add mushrooms, thyme, salt, and pepper and cook, stirring occasionally, 10 minutes longer, or until mushrooms are tender and liquid has evaporated.
3. In shallow 2½-quart baking dish, combine orzo, rice, and mushroom mixture and stir until blended. Cool slightly. Cover and refrigerate up to 2 days, if not serving right away.
4. To serve, preheat oven to 350°F. Cover orzo mixture and bake 45 minutes, or until hot.

1¼ cups orzo pasta (about 8 ounces)
1 cup wild rice (about 6 ounces)
3 tablespoons butter or margarine
1 small onion, finely chopped
1 medium celery stalk, finely chopped
1 pound medium mushrooms, trimmed and sliced
2 teaspoons chopped fresh thyme
1 teaspoon salt
¼ teaspoon coarsely ground black pepper
thyme sprigs for garnish

**Each serving:** About 155 calories, 5 g protein, 26 g carbohydrate, 3 g total fat (1 g saturated), 0 mg cholesterol, 220 mg sodium.

◀ WILD RICE
AND ORZO PILAF
AND LEEKS
VINAIGRETTE

◆

# Leeks Vinaigrette

16 slender leeks (4½ to 5
  pounds)
2¼ teaspoons salt
2 tablespoons red wine vinegar
2 teaspoons Dijon mustard
¼ teaspoon ground black pepper
¼ cup olive oil
2 tablespoons chopped fresh
  parsley

**Each serving:** About 105 calories,
1 g protein, 11 g carbohydrate,
7 g total fat (1 g saturated),
0 mg cholesterol, 180 mg sodium.

**Prep:** 20 minutes  ◆  **Cook:** 10 minutes
**Makes** 8 accompaniment servings

1. In 8-quart Dutch oven, heat *5 quarts water* to boiling over high heat. Meanwhile, cut root ends from leeks. Trim leeks to 6 inches; discard tops (or save for another use). Cut leeks lengthwise almost in half down to beginning of white part, keeping bottom 2 to 3 inches intact. Remove any bruised or tough dark-green outer leaves. Rinse leeks thoroughly with cold running water, fanning cut part, to remove all sand.

2. Add leeks and 2 teaspoons salt to Dutch oven; cook 10 minutes, or until tender when pierced with knife. With slotted spoon, transfer leeks to colander to drain; rinse with cold running water. Drain again and pat dry with paper towels.

3. Coarsely chop any loose pieces of leek and spread on platter; arrange leeks in a row, in a single layer, on top. Cover leeks and refrigerate up to 24 hours, if not serving right away.

4. *Prepare vinaigrette:* In small bowl, with wire whisk or fork, mix vinegar, mustard, pepper, and remaining ¼ teaspoon salt until blended. In thin, steady stream, gradually whisk in oil. Pour vinaigrette into small jar; cover tightly and refrigerate until ready to serve.

5. Serve leeks at room temperature. Spoon vinaigrette evenly over leeks; sprinkle with parsley.

# Spinach and Potato Gratin

**Prep:** 40 minutes   ◆   **Bake:** 1 hour 30 minutes
**Makes** 12 accompaniment servings

1. Preheat oven to 350°F. Grease shallow 3-quart casserole.
2. In 10-inch skillet, melt butter over medium heat. Add shallots and cook, stirring occasionally, 5 minutes, or until tender. Remove skillet from heat; stir in spinach, nutmeg, ¼ teaspoon salt, and ¼ teaspoon pepper.
3. Arrange one-third of potato slices, overlapping, in casserole. Top with one-third of cheese and one-half of spinach mixture. Repeat layering with remaining ingredients, ending with cheese.
4. In 4-cup measuring cup or large bowl, with wire whisk, mix milk, cream, cornstarch, remaining ¾ teaspoon salt, and ¼ teaspoon pepper until smooth. Pour milk mixture evenly over casserole.
5. Place sheet of foil underneath casserole; crimp foil edges to form a rim to catch any overflow during baking. Cover and bake 30 minutes. Remove cover and bake 1 hour longer, or until center is hot and bubbly and top is golden.

1 tablespoon butter or margarine
3 large shallots, thinly sliced
2 packages (10 ounces each) frozen chopped spinach, thawed and squeezed dry
⅛ teaspoon ground nutmeg
1 teaspoon salt
½ teaspoon coarsely ground black pepper
9 medium all-purpose potatoes (3 pounds), peeled and cut into ¼-inch-thick slices
4 ounces Gruyère cheese, shredded (1 cup)
1½ cups milk
1 cup heavy or whipping cream
1 tablespoon cornstarch

**Each serving:** About 230 calories, 8 g protein, 24 g carbohydrate, 13 g total fat (7 g saturated), 42 mg cholesterol, 315 mg sodium.

# Sweet Potato and Apple Gratin

**Prep:** 40 minutes  ◆  **Bake:** 1 hour
**Makes** 8 accompaniment servings

## Sweet-Potato Layers

2 tablespoons butter or margarine

3 large Golden Delicious apples
  (1¼ pounds), peeled, cored,
  and cut into ¼-inch-thick
  slices

1 large onion (12 ounces), cut
  in half and thinly sliced

2 tablespoons applejack brandy
  or Calvados

6 medium sweet potatoes
  (2½ pounds)

¾ teaspoon salt

¼ teaspoon coarsely ground
  black pepper

¼ teaspoon ground nutmeg

1 cup apple cider or apple juice

## Pecan-Crumb Topping

2 tablespoons butter or margarine

3 slices firm white bread, cut into
  ¼-inch pieces (1¾ cups)

½ cup pecans, coarsely chopped

**Each serving:** About 300 calories,
4 g protein, 50 g carbohydrate,
11 g total fat (2 g saturated),
0 mg cholesterol, 335 mg sodium.

1. *Prepare sweet-potato layers:* Grease shallow 2½-quart casserole. In 12-inch skillet, melt butter over medium heat. Add apples and onion and cook, stirring frequently, about 25 minutes, until tender and golden. Stir in applejack; cook 1 minute. Remove skillet from heat.

2. Meanwhile, peel and thinly slice sweet potatoes. In cup, mix salt, pepper, and nutmeg.

3. Arrange one-third of sweet potato slices, overlapping, in casserole. Spoon one-third of apple mixture over potatoes. Sprinkle with one-third salt mixture. Repeat layering 2 more times. Pour apple cider over potato and apple layers. Cover with foil and refrigerate up to 24 hours, if not serving right away.

4. *Prepare topping:* In nonstick 10-inch skillet, melt butter over medium heat. Add bread pieces and pecans and cook, stirring occasionally, 5 to 6 minutes, until bread and pecans are lightly toasted. Cool topping completely. Transfer topping to small container; cover and set aside, up to 24 hours.

5. To serve, preheat oven to 400°F. Cover casserole with foil and bake 1 hour. Remove foil; sprinkle casserole with topping just before serving.

◆ SWEET POTATO ▶
AND APPLE GRATIN

◆

# Roasted Red and White Potatoes with Garlic

**Prep:** 15 minutes  ◆  **Roast:** 1 hour 25 minutes
**Makes** 10 accompaniment servings

1. Preheat oven to 325°F. Place potatoes and red onions in large roasting pan (17" by 11½"). Add oil, salt, thyme, pepper, and garlic and toss to coat evenly. Roast 1 hour on lower rack of oven.
2. Turn oven control to 450°F and roast potatoes, turning occasionally with spatula, 25 minutes longer, until golden and fork-tender. Garnish with fresh thyme sprigs.

4½ pounds medium red and all-purpose potatoes, unpeeled and each cut into quarters
2 medium red onions, each cut into 6 wedges
¼ cup olive oil
1¼ teaspoons salt
1 teaspoon dried thyme
½ teaspoon coarsely ground black pepper
2 garlic cloves, crushed with garlic press
fresh thyme sprigs for garnish

**Each serving:** About 210 calories, 5 g protein, 36 g carbohydrate, 6 g total fat (1 g saturated), 0 mg cholesterol, 280 mg sodium.

# Hoppin' John

**Prep:** 15 minutes  ◆  **Cook:** 20 minutes
**Makes** 20 accompaniment servings

1. In 4-quart saucepan, heat oil over medium-high heat. Add celery, onion, and red pepper; cook 10 minutes, or until golden. Add garlic; cook 2 minutes longer.
2. Rinse peas with cold running water and discard any stones or shriveled peas. Add peas, ham hock, broth, crushed red pepper, bay leaf, 1 teaspoon salt, and water to celery mixture; heat to boiling over high heat. Reduce heat; cover and simmer 40 minutes, or until peas are tender.
3. Meanwhile, prepare rice as label directs, but use remaining 1 teaspoon salt and do not add butter.
4. In large bowl, gently mix pea mixture and rice. Serve hot. Garnish with chopped parsley, if you like.

1 tablespoon vegetable oil
2 celery stalks, chopped
1 large onion, chopped
1 medium red pepper, chopped
2 garlic cloves, finely chopped
1 package (16 ounces) dried black-eyed peas
1 large smoked ham hock (¾ pound)
2 cans (14½ ounces each) chicken broth
¼ teaspoon crushed red pepper
1 bay leaf
2 teaspoons salt
4 cups water
2 cups regular long-grain rice
chopped parsley for garnish (optional)

**Each serving:** About 150 calories, 8 g protein, 26 g carbohydrate, 2 g total fat (0 g saturated), 9 mg cholesterol, 455 mg sodium.

# Mashed Potatoes with Sauerkraut

**Prep:** 15 minutes ◆ **Cook:** 40 to 45 minutes
**Makes** 14 accompaniment servings

### Sauerkraut Topping

4 tablespoons butter or margarine

4 medium onions, thinly sliced

2 packages (16 ounces each) sauerkraut, rinsed and squeezed dry

1 can (14½ ounces) chicken broth

2 medium Golden Delicious apples, peeled, cored, and grated

½ teaspoon caraway seeds

### Mashed Potatoes

15 medium all-purpose potatoes (5 pounds), peeled and cut into 1-inch chunks

1¼ teaspoons salt

1¼ cups milk, warmed

½ cup butter or margarine (1 stick)

**Each serving:** About 245 calories, 5 g protein, 34 g carbohydrate, 11 g total fat (2 g saturated), 3 mg cholesterol, 610 mg sodium.

1. *Prepare topping:* In 12-inch skillet, melt butter over medium heat. Add onions and cook, stirring occasionally, about 15 minutes, until tender and lightly browned. Add sauerkraut, broth, apples, and caraway seeds; heat to boiling over high heat. Reduce heat; cover and simmer 40 to 45 minutes, until sauerkraut is tender. Keep warm.

2. Meanwhile, prepare mashed potatoes: In 8-quart Dutch oven, combine potatoes and enough *water* to cover; heat to boiling over high heat. Reduce heat; cover and simmer 15 minutes, or until potatoes are fork-tender. Drain.

3. Return potatoes to Dutch oven. With potato masher, mash potatoes with salt. Add warmed milk and butter; mash until mixture is well blended. Spoon potatoes into serving bowl; top with sauerkraut.

# Italian Sausage Stuffing

**Prep:** 25 minutes ◆ **Bake:** 30 minutes
**Makes** about 12 cups

1 pound sweet Italian-sausage links, casings removed

1 package (14 to 16 ounces) herb-seasoned stuffing mix

½ cup butter or margarine (1 stick)

2 large celery stalks, finely chopped

1 medium onion, finely chopped

2½ cups hot water

**Each ½ cup:** About 175 calories, 4 g protein, 16 g carbohydrate, 10 g total fat (3 g saturated), 15 mg cholesterol, 480 mg sodium.

1. Preheat oven to 325°F. Heat 10-inch skillet over medium-high heat until hot. Add sausage and cook, stirring frequently to break up sausage, about 10 minutes, until browned. With slotted spoon, transfer sausage to large bowl; stir in stuffing mix.

2. To drippings in skillet, add butter; heat until melted. Add celery and onion and cook, stirring occasionally, about 10 minutes, until vegetables are tender and golden. Transfer celery mixture to bowl with sausage.

3. Pour hot water over stuffing mixture; toss to mix well. Spoon stuffing into 13" by 9" glass baking dish; cover with foil and bake 30 minutes, or until stuffing is heated through.

ITALIAN
SAUSAGE
STUFFING
♦

# Classic Bread Stuffing

**Prep:** 25 minutes    ♦    **Bake:** 45 minutes

**Makes** about 10 cups stuffing

1. In 5-quart Dutch oven, melt butter over medium heat. Add celery and onion and cook, stirring occasionally, about 15 minutes, until tender.

2. Remove Dutch oven from heat. Add bread cubes, broth, parsley, thyme, salt, pepper, and sage; toss to combine well. Use to stuff 12- to 16-pound turkey, or serve in baking dish alongside poultry or ham: Spoon stuffing into greased 13" by 9" baking dish; cover with foil and bake in preheated 325°F. oven about 45 minutes until heated through.

*Tip:* Remember that the stuffing is only being heated through while inside the bird and does not actually cook. Therefore, it is important that the ingredients are thoroughly cooked before being combined. To save time, cut up the raw stuffing ingredients the night before, then cover and refrigerate. Stuff the bird just before roasting—never in advance—and roast immediately. Lightly stuff the body and neck cavities.  Do not pack; the stuffing needs room to expand during cooking. (Bake the extra stuffing in a covered buttered baking dish thirty minutes or until heated through.) After cooking, the stuffing temperature should have reached 160°F to be safe. If the poultry has reached the correct temperature but the stuffing hasn't, transfer the stuffing to a buttered baking dish and continue baking until 160°F is reached. Leftover stuffing should be promptly removed from the bird to avoid potential bacterial growth.

½ cup butter or margarine
  (1 stick)
5 celery stalks, finely chopped
1 medium onion, finely chopped
2 loaves (16 ounces each) sliced
  firm white bread; cut into
  ¾-inch cubes
1 can (14½ ounces) chicken broth
¼ cup chopped fresh parsley
1 teaspoon dried thyme
¾ teaspoon salt
½ teaspoon ground black pepper
½ teaspoon dried sage

**Each ½ cup:** About 170 calories, 4 g protein, 24 g carbohydrate, 6 g total fat (3 g saturated), 1 g fiber, 13 mg cholesterol, 475 mg sodium.

# New England Apple-Nut Stuffing

½ cup butter or margarine
   (1 stick)
3 large celery stalks, finely
   chopped
1 large onion, chopped
3 medium Golden Delicious
   apples (1 pound), peeled,
   cored, and finely chopped
1½ loaves (24 ounces) sliced firm
   white bread, cut into ¾-inch
   cubes and lightly toasted
1 can (14½ ounces) chicken broth
½ cup pecans, toasted and
   chopped
½ cup walnuts, toasted and
   chopped
2 tablespoons sesame seeds,
   toasted (optional)
½ teaspoon poultry seasoning
¼ teaspoon dried oregano leaves,
   crumbled
¼ teaspoon coarsely ground
   black pepper

**Each ½ cup:** About 155 calories,
3 g protein, 18 g carbohydrate,
8 g total fat (1 g saturated),
0 mg cholesterol, 255 mg sodium.

**Prep:** 45 minutes    ◆    **Bake:** 45 minutes
**Makes** about 12 cups

1. Preheat oven to 325°F. In 12-inch skillet, melt butter over medium heat. Add celery and onion and cook, stirring occasionally, 10 minutes, or until tender. Add apples and cook 5 minutes longer.
2. In large bowl, combine celery mixture with toasted bread cubes and remaining ingredients; toss to mix well. Spoon stuffing into greased 13" by 9" glass baking dish; cover with foil and bake 45 minutes, or until heated through.

# Cranberry-Pear Relish

**Prep:** 5 minutes plus chilling ◆ **Cook:** 12 to 14 minutes
**Makes** about 3 cups

In 3-quart saucepan, combine cranberries, sugar, vinegar, and water and heat to boiling over high heat, stirring occasionally. Reduce heat; simmer, uncovered, 8 minutes, or until most of cranberries have popped. Add pear; cover and cook 2 to 3 minutes longer. Cover and refrigerate relish about 4 hours, until well chilled. If you like, transfer relish to airtight container and refrigerate up to 2 days.

1 bag (12 ounces) cranberries
  (3 cups)
1¼ cups packed brown sugar
¼ cup balsamic vinegar
½ cup water
1 medium pear, peeled, cored,
  and finely chopped

**Each ¼ cup:** About 115 calories, 0 g protein, 29 g carbohydrate, 0 g total fat (0 g saturated), 0 mg cholesterol, 10 mg sodium.

# No-Cook Cranberry-Orange Relish

**Prep:** 15 minutes plus chilling
**Makes** about 3 cups

In food processor with knife blade attached, combine all ingredients and process until mixture is coarsely chopped. Cover and refrigerate relish about 2 hours, until well chilled. If you like, transfer relish to an airtight container and refrigerate up to 2 days.

*Tip:* Condiments really perk up the palate—their sharp, sweet, and savory flavors enliven many a dish. But with varied textures and glistening jewel-like colors, they're also a feast for the eyes.

1 bag (12 ounces) cranberries
  (3 cups)
1 medium orange, cut up
½ cup dark seedless raisins
½ cup sugar

**Each ¼ cup:** About 70 calories, 1 g protein, 18 g carbohydrate, 0 g total fat (0 g saturated), 0 mg cholesterol, 10 mg sodium.

◀ CRANBERRY-FIG CHUTNEY,
CRANBERRY-PEAR RELISH, AND
NO-COOK CRANBERRY-ORANGE RELISH
*( from top )*

◆

# Cranberry-Fig Chutney

**Prep:** 15 minutes plus chilling  ◆  **Cook:** 35 minutes
**Makes** about 4 cups

1 bag (12 ounces) cranberries
   (3 cups)
1 package (8-ounces) dried
   Calimyrna figs, sliced
1 small onion, chopped
½ small lemon, chopped
1 cup packed brown sugar
⅓ cup red wine vinegar
2 tablespoons minced, peeled
   fresh ginger
½ teaspoon salt
¼ teaspoon coarsely ground
   black pepper
1 cup water

In 3-quart saucepan, heat all ingredients to boiling over medium-high heat. Reduce heat; simmer, uncovered, stirring occasionally, 30 minutes. Cover and refrigerate chutney about 4 hours, until well chilled. If you like, transfer chutney to an airtight container and refrigerate up to 2 days.

**Each ¼ cup:** About 105 calories, 1 g protein, 27 g carbohydrate, 0 g total fat (0 g saturated), 0 mg cholesterol, 75 mg sodium.

# Dried Apricot, Prune, and Cherry Compote

**Prep:** 10 minutes plus cooling  ◆  **Cook:** 8 minutes
**Makes** 10 servings

4 cups apple cider or apple juice
8 ounces (1 cup) dried apricots,
   each cut into 3 strips
¼ cup packed light brown sugar
3 strips (3" by 1" each)
   lemon peel
1 cinnamon stick (3 inches)
8 ounces (1 cup) pitted prunes,
   each cut in half
4 ounces (½ cup) dried tart
   cherries
½ teaspoon vanilla extract

1. In 3-quart saucepan, combine apple cider, apricots, brown sugar, lemon peel, and cinnamon stick and heat to boiling over high heat. Reduce heat; simmer, uncovered, 5 minutes.
2. Spoon mixture into large bowl; stir in prunes, dried cherries, and vanilla. Serve at room temperature or cover with plastic wrap and refrigerate. Store in refrigerator up to 1 week.

**Each serving:** About 175 calories, 2 g protein, 46 g carbohydrate, 1 g total fat (0 g saturated), 0 mg cholesterol, 7 mg sodium.

*Salads*

▲ HARVEST
SALAD P.57

# Winter Salad with Ripe Pears and Toasted Pecans

**Prep:** 45 minutes

**Makes** 10 accompaniment servings

1. In very large bowl, with wire whisk or fork, mix vinegar, mustard, salt, and pepper until blended. In thin, steady stream, gradually whisk in oil until mixture thickens slightly. Add pear wedges; toss to coat pears with dressing.
2. With vegetable peeler, shave 1 cup loosely packed shavings from wedge of Parmesan cheese; set aside.
3. Add radicchio, endive, and arugula to bowl with pears; toss to coat evenly. Serve salad topped with Parmesan shavings and pecans.

3 tablespoons red wine vinegar
2 teaspoons Dijon mustard
½ teaspoon salt
½ teaspoon coarsely ground black pepper
⅓ cup olive oil
3 medium, ripe pears; peeled, cored, and each cut into 16 wedges
1 wedge Parmesan cheese (4 ounces)
2 small heads radicchio (7 ounces each), torn into large pieces
2 small heads Belgian endive, separated into leaves
2 bunches arugula (4 ounces each), trimmed
½ cup pecans, toasted and coarsely chopped

**Each serving:** About 205 calories, 7 g protein, 14 g carbohydrate, 15 g total fat (3 g saturated), 9 mg cholesterol, 360 mg sodium.

# Mesclun Salad with Parmesan Polenta Rounds

**Prep:** 20 minutes ◆ **Broil:** 6 to 8 minutes
**Makes** 6 first-course servings

1. Preheat broiler. Arrange polenta slices in a single layer on nonstick cookie sheet. In small bowl, mix Parmesan, ¼ teaspoon salt, ¼ teaspoon pepper, and thyme. Sprinkle 1 teaspoon cheese mixture on top of each polenta slice. Place cookie sheet in broiler at closest position to source of heat; broil polenta 6 to 8 minutes, until cheese melts and top is golden.
2. Meanwhile, in large bowl, whisk vinegars, oil, mayonnaise, mustard, sugar, remaining ¼ teaspoon salt, and ¼ teaspoon pepper until blended. Add salad greens and toss until evenly coated.
3. To serve, divide salad greens among 6 salad plates. Top each salad with 3 warm polenta rounds.

1 log (16 ounces) precooked polenta, cut into 18 slices
2 ounces Parmesan cheese, coarsely grated (½ cup)
½ teaspoon salt
½ teaspoon coarsely gound black pepper
¼ teaspoon dried thyme
1 tablespoon white wine vinegar
1 tablespoon balsamic vinegar
1 tablespoon olive oil
1 tablespoon light mayonnaise
½ teaspoon Dijon mustard
¼ teaspoon sugar
2 bags (about 5 ounces each) mesclun salad greens

**Each serving:** About 135 calories, 6 g protein, 14 g carbohydrate, 6 g total fat (2 g saturated), 2 g fiber, 8 mg cholesterol, 630 mg sodium.

# Spinach and Tangerine Salad

**Prep:** 30 minutes
**Makes** 8 first-course servings

1. From 1 tangerine, grate peel. Cut remaining peel and pith from all tangerines; discard. Cut each tangerine in half, then cut each half crosswise into ¼-inch-thick slices. Tear spinach and Bibb lettuce into bite-size pieces.
2. In large bowl, with wire whisk or fork, mix oil, vinegar, sugar, mustard, salt, pepper, and grated peel. Add spinach, lettuce, and tangerine slices; toss well.

*Tip:* Washing greens is an easy do-ahead task. Tear into bite-size pieces by hand (a knife blade may bruise leaves), soak briefly, and spin or pat dry. Wrap in paper towels, then enclose in plastic bags. Place in your crisper. Use within two or three days.

4 medium tangerines or small oranges
1 large bunch (1 pound) spinach, tough stems trimmed
2 small heads Bibb lettuce (8 ounces)
3 tablespoons extravirgin olive oil
3 tablespoons cider vinegar
1 teaspoon sugar
1 teaspoon Dijon mustard
⅛ teaspoon salt
⅛ teaspoon coarsely ground black pepper

**Each serving:** About 80 calories, 2 g protein, 8 g carbohydrate, 5 g total fat (1 g saturated), 0 mg cholesterol, 95 mg sodium.

◄ *M*ESCLUN SALAD WITH PARMESAN
POLENTA ROUNDS

◆

◢ BEET,
ORANGE, AND
WATERCRESS
SALAD
◆

# Beet, Orange, and Watercress Salad

**Prep:** 45 minutes ◆ **Cook:** 30 minutes
**Makes** 10 accompaniment servings

2 pounds beets without tops
  (10 medium beets)
4 large oranges
¼ cup red wine vinegar
1 tablespoon Dijon mustard
1 teaspoon sugar
¾ teaspoon salt
¼ teaspoon coarsely ground
  black pepper
¼ cup olive oil
3 bunches watercress (4 ounces
  each), tough stems discarded
1 medium red onion, thinly sliced

Each serving: About 110 calories,
3 g protein, 15 g carbohydrate,
6 g total fat (1 g saturated),
0 mg cholesterol, 250 mg sodium.

1. In 4-quart saucepan, heat beets and enough *water* to cover over high heat, to boiling. Reduce heat; cover and simmer 30 minutes, or until beets are fork-tender.

2. Meanwhile, from 1 orange, grate 1 teaspoon peel. Cut remaining peel and pith from all oranges; discard. Holding oranges over large bowl to catch juice, cut out sections between membranes. Place sections in small bowl; set aside. Into juice, with wire whisk or fork, mix vinegar, mustard, sugar, salt, pepper, and grated peel until blended. In thin, steady stream, gradually whisk in oil.

3. Drain beets and cool with cold running water. Peel and cut each beet in half, then cut each half into ¼-inch-thick slices.

4. To dressing in bowl, add beets, orange sections, watercress, and red onion; toss to coat.

# Harvest Salad

**Prep:** 15 minutes
**Makes** 8 first-course servings

1. In a large bowl, with wire whisk or fork, mix vinegar, oil, salt, and pepper until blended. Add salad greens and cherries; toss until evenly coated.
2. To serve, divide greens among 8 salad plates; sprinkle each with cheese and pumpkin seeds. Garnish with cherry tomatoes.

3 tablespoons raspberry or
   balsamic vinegar
2 tablespoons olive oil
¼ teaspoon salt
¼ teaspoon ground black pepper
2 bags (10 ounces each)
   European-style salad greens
½ cup dried tart cherries
4 ounces blue cheese, crumbled
   (½ cup)
⅓ cup roasted, salted
   pumpkin seeds
red and yellow cherry tomatoes
   for garnish

**Each serving:** About 170 calories, 7 g protein, 11 g carbohydrate, 11 g total fat (4 g saturated), 3 g fiber, 11 mg cholesterol, 335 mg sodium.

◀ *H*ARVEST SALAD
◆

▲ CHOCOLATE
CHERRY COFFEE
CAKE P. 62

# Holiday Brunch

## Bread Pudding with Warm Banana-Maple Sauce

1 loaf unsliced rich egg bread,
 such as challah (1 pound),
 cut into 1-inch-thick slices
3 cups milk
½ teaspoon salt
10 large eggs
¼ cup plus 1 tablespoon sugar
1 teaspoon ground cinnamon
4 tablespoons butter or margarine
6 medium firm bananas, cut into
 ¼-inch-thick slices
1 bottle (8 ounces) maple syrup

**Each serving with sauce:** About
365 calories, 11 g protein,
52 g carbohydrate, 13 g total fat
(4 g saturated), 205 mg
cholesterol, 410 mg sodium.

**Prep:** 20 minutes plus overnight    •    **Bake:** 45 minutes
**Makes** 12 main-dish servings

1. Grease shallow 3½- to 4-quart ceramic casserole or 13" by 9" glass baking dish. Arrange bread slices, overlapping slightly, in dish.

2. In medium bowl, with wire whisk or fork, beat milk, salt, eggs, and ¼ cup sugar until well mixed. Slowly pour egg mixture over bread slices; prick bread slices with fork and press slices down to absorb egg mixture. Spoon any egg mixture that bread has not absorbed over bread slices.

3. In cup, mix cinnamon with remaining 1 tablespoon sugar; sprinkle over top of bread pudding and dot with 2 tablespoons butter. Cover and refrigerate at least 30 minutes or overnight.

4. Preheat oven to 325°F. Remove cover from bread pudding and bake 45 minutes, or until knife inserted in center comes out clean.

5. *Meanwhile, prepare banana sauce:* In nonstick 12-inch skillet, melt remaining 2 tablespoons butter over medium-high heat. Add banana slices and cook about 3 minutes, until lightly browned. Pour maple syrup over bananas; heat to boiling. Boil 2 to 3 minutes, until mixture thickens slightly. Serve warm sauce in bowl with bread pudding.

*Bread Pudding with Warm Banana-Maple* ▶
*Sauce, and Orange-Cranberry Fizz*

# Orange-Cranberry Fizz

**Prep:** 10 minutes
**Makes** about 10 cups or 10 servings

1 quart cranberry-raspberry
   juice blend, chilled
2 cups cranberry or plain
   ginger ale, chilled
2 cups orange juice
2 cups lemon-lime seltzer, chilled
orange and lime slices, and
   cranberries for garnish
   (optional)

In large pitcher (about 3 quarts), mix cranberry-raspberry juice, ginger ale, and orange juice. Refrigerate until ready to serve. Just before serving, stir in seltzer. Garnish with orange and lime slices, and cranberries, if you like.

**Each serving:** About 95 calories, 0 g protein, 24 g carbohydrate, 0 g total fat (0 g saturated), 0 mg cholesterol, 20 mg sodium.

# Oven-Baked Pepper Bacon

**Prep:** 10 minutes   ◆   **Bake:** 25 minutes
**Makes** 12 accompaniment servings

1½ pounds sliced lean bacon
2½ teaspoons coarsely ground
   black pepper

1. Preheat oven to 400°F. Arrange bacon slices in 2 jelly-roll or shallow roasting pans, overlapping the lean edge of each slice with the fat edge of the next.
2. Evenly sprinkle pepper over bacon slices. Place pans on 2 oven racks and bake 25 minutes, switching pans between upper and lower racks halfway through baking, or until bacon is golden brown and crisp. Transfer bacon to paper towels to drain; keep warm.

**Each serving:** About 90 calories, 5 g protein, 0 g carbohydrate, 8 g total fat (3 g saturated), 13 mg cholesterol, 255 mg sodium.

◀ *P*UFFY ▶
CHEDDAR GRITS
AND OVEN-BAKED
PEPPER BACON
◆

# Puffy Cheddar Grits

**Prep:** 20 minutes ◆ **Bake:** 45 minutes
**Makes** 12 main-dish servings

1. Preheat oven to 325°F. In 3-quart saucepan, combine butter, salt, 1½ cups milk, and water and heat to boiling over medium-high heat. Gradually stir in grits, beating constantly with wire whisk to prevent lumps. Reduce heat; cover and cook, stirring occasionally, 5 minutes. (Grits will be very stiff.) Remove saucepan from heat; blend in cheese.
2. In large bowl, with wire whisk or fork, mix hot pepper sauce, pepper, eggs, and remaining 2 cups milk until blended. Gradually stir grits mixture into egg mixture.
3. Grease shallow 2½-quart casserole. Pour grits mixture into casserole. Bake, uncovered, 45 minutes, or until knife inserted in center comes out clean.

2 tablespoons butter or margarine
1 teaspoon salt
3½ cups milk
2 cups water
1¼ cups quick-cooking grits
1 package (8 ounces) shredded
   Cheddar cheese (2 cups)
1 teaspoon hot pepper sauce
¼ teaspoon pepper
5 large eggs

**Each serving:** About 230 calories, 12 g protein, 17 g carbohydrate, 13 g total fat (7 g saturated), 118 mg cholesterol, 385 mg sodium.

# Festive Christmas Tree Rolls

**Prep:** 45 minutes plus rising and cooling ◆ **Bake:** 20 to 25 minutes
**Makes** 25 rolls

1. In large bowl, combine yeast, granulated sugar, cardamom, 1½ cups flour, and 1½ teaspoons salt. In 1-quart saucepan, heat butter and 1 cup water over low heat until very warm (120° to 130°F). Butter does not need to melt completely.
2. With mixer at low speed, gradually beat liquid into dry ingredients just until blended. Increase speed to medium; beat 2 minutes, occasionally scraping bowl with rubber spatula. Beat in 1 egg, 1 egg yolk, and ½ cup flour to make a thick batter; continue beating 2 minutes, scraping bowl often. Reserve remaining egg white. With wooden spoon, stir in 2½ cups flour to make a soft dough.
3. Turn dough onto lightly floured surface and knead until smooth and elastic, about 10 minutes, working in more flour (about ¼ cup) if needed to keep dough from sticking to work surface. Shape dough into a ball; place in greased large bowl, turning dough to grease top. Cover; let rise in warm place (80° to 85°F) about 1 hour, until doubled.
4. Punch down dough. Knead in raisins and candied fruit. Cut dough into 25 equal pieces; let rest 15 minutes for easier shaping. Shape into balls.

2 packages active dry yeast
¼ cup granulated sugar
1½ teaspoons ground cardamom
about 4¾ cups all-purpose flour
1½ plus ⅛ teaspoons salt
½ cup butter or margarine
   (1 stick)
1 cup plus 1 tablespoon water
2 large eggs
½ cup golden raisins
½ cup diced mixed candied fruit
¾ cup confectioners' sugar

**Each roll:** About 180 calories, 3 g protein, 32 g carbohydrate, 4 g total fat (1 g saturated), 17 mg cholesterol, 195 mg sodium.

5. To make Christmas tree, place 1 dough ball at top of lightly greased large cookie sheet. Make a second row by centering 2 dough balls directly under the first ball and placing balls ¼ inch apart to allow space for rising. Continue making rows by increasing each row by 1 ball and centering balls directly under previous row, until there are 6 rows in all. Leave space to allow for rising. Use last 4 balls to make trunk of tree. Cover and let rise about 40 minutes, until doubled.

6. Preheat oven to 375°F. In cup, with fork, beat reserved egg white with remaining ⅛ teaspoon salt. Brush rolls with egg white. Bake rolls 20 to 25 minutes, until golden and rolls sound hollow when lightly tapped. With wide spatula, transfer rolls to wire rack to cool, about 1 hour.

7. When cool, prepare glaze: In bowl, mix confectioners' sugar and remaining 1 tablespoon water. With spoon, drizzle glaze in zigzag pattern over tree.

# Chocolate-Cherry Coffee Cake

**Prep:** 30 minutes plus cooling    ◆    **Bake:** 1 hour 10 minutes
**Makes** 16 servings

½ cup semisweet chocolate
    mini pieces
1 tablespoon unsweetened cocoa
2 teaspoons ground cinnamon
1⅔ cups granulated sugar
¾ cup butter or margarine,
    softened (1½ sticks)
3 cups all-purpose flour
1½ teaspoons baking soda
1½ teaspoons baking powder
2 teaspoons vanilla extract
½ teaspoon salt
1 container (16 ounces) light
    sour cream
3 large eggs
⅔ cup dried cherries
confectioners' sugar for garnish
    (optional)

**Each serving:** About 335 calories, 5 g protein, 49 g carbohydrate, 13 g total fat (2 g saturated), 49 mg cholesterol, 370 mg sodium.

1. Preheat oven to 325°F. Grease and flour 10-inch Bundt pan. In small bowl, combine chocolate mini pieces, cocoa, cinnamon, and ⅓ cup granulated sugar; set aside.

2. In large bowl, with mixer at low speed, beat butter and remaining 1⅓ cups granulated sugar until blended. Increase speed to medium; beat 2 minutes, occasionally scraping bowl with rubber spatula.

3. Reduce speed to low. Add flour, baking soda, baking powder, vanilla extract, salt, sour cream, and eggs; beat until well mixed. Increase speed to medium; beat 2 minutes, scraping bowl. Stir in dried cherries.

4. Spread one-third of batter in Bundt pan; sprinkle with half the chocolate mixture. Top with half the remaining batter; sprinkle with remaining chocolate mixture. Spread remaining batter on top.

5. Bake coffee cake 1 hour 10 minutes, or until toothpick inserted in center of cake comes out clean. Cool cake in pan on wire rack 10 minutes. Invert cake onto wire rack to cool completely.

6. Sift confectioners' sugar over cake before serving, if you like.

CHOCOLATE-
CHERRY
COFFEE CAKE AND
HOLIDAY FRUIT
COMPOTE
◆

# Holiday Fruit Compote

**Prep:** 30 minutes plus chilling  ◆  **Cook:** 15 minutes
**Makes** 12 servings

1. From 1 orange, remove 1-inch-wide continuous strip of peel. In 2-quart saucepan, combine orange peel, sugar, lemon juice, cinnamon stick, and water and heat to boiling over medium-high heat. Reduce heat; cover and simmer 15 minutes, or until syrup thickens slightly. Remove pan from heat. Add apple and pear wedges; let stand 30 minutes at room temperature to soften fruit slightly.

2. Meanwhile, from 1 remaining orange, cut peel into thin strips; wrap with plastic wrap and refrigerate for garnish later. Cut peel from grapefruits and remaining orange and discard. Holding oranges and grapefruits over medium bowl to catch juice, cut sections from between membranes and add to bowl.

3. Add apple mixture to orange and grapefruit sections; cover and refrigerate until well chilled, at least 4 hours or overnight. To serve, garnish with orange-peel strips.

3 medium oranges
1¼ cups sugar
2 tablespoons lemon juice
1 cinnamon stick (3 inches)
2 cups water
1 medium red eating apple, unpeeled, cored, and cut into thin wedges
1 medium pear, unpeeled, cored, and cut into thin wedges
3 medium pink or red grapefruits

**Each serving:** About 135 calories, 1 g protein, 35 g carbohydrate, 0 g total fat (0 g saturated), 0 mg cholesterol, 1 mg sodium.

▲ NEW ENGLAND
BROWN BREAD P. 65

# Breads

## Refrigerator Potato Rolls

**Prep:** 1 hour 30 minutes plus rising and overnight to chill
**Bake:** 25 minutes    ◆    **Makes** 2 dozen rolls

3 medium all-purpose potatoes
 (1 pound), peeled and cut
 into 1-inch pieces
2 tablespoons sugar
1 tablespoon salt
2 packages quick-rise yeast
about 9¾ cups all-purpose flour
4 tablespoons butter or
 margarine
2 large eggs

**Each roll:** About 225 calories,
6 g protein, 43 g carbohydrate,
3 g total fat (1 g saturated),
18 mg cholesterol, 300 mg
sodium.

1. In 2-quart saucepan, heat potatoes and *4 cups water* to boiling over high heat. Reduce heat; cover and simmer 15 minutes, or until potatoes are fork-tender. Drain potatoes, reserving 2 cups potato cooking water. Return potatoes to saucepan. With potato masher, mash potatoes until smooth; set aside.

2. In large bowl, combine sugar, salt, yeast, and 3 cups flour. In 1-quart saucepan, combine butter and reserved potato water and heat over low heat until very warm (120° to 130°F). Butter does not need to melt completely.

3. With mixer at low speed, gradually beat warm liquid into dry ingredients just until blended. Increase speed to medium; beat 2 minutes, occasionally scraping bowl with rubber spatula. Gradually beat in 1 egg, 1 egg yolk, and 1 cup flour to make a thick batter; continue beating 2 minutes, scraping bowl often. Refrigerate remaining egg white to brush on rolls later. With wooden spoon, stir in mashed potatoes, then 5 cups flour, 1 cup at a time, to make a soft dough. (You may want to transfer mixture to a larger bowl for easier mixing.)

4. Turn dough onto well-floured surface and knead until smooth and elastic, about 10 minutes, working in more flour (about ¾ cup) while kneading. Cut dough into 24 equal pieces; cover and let rest 15 minutes. Grease large roasting pan (17" by 11½").

5. Shape dough into balls and place in roasting pan. Cover pan with plastic wrap and refrigerate overnight. (You can bake rolls the same day. After shaping into balls, cover and let rise in warm place about 40 minutes, until doubled, then bake as directed in step 7.)

6. When ready to bake, remove plastic wrap; cover with towel and let rise in warm place (80° to 85°F) about 30 minutes, until doubled.

7. Preheat oven to 400°F. With fork, beat reserved egg white. Brush rolls with egg white. Bake rolls 25 to 30 minutes, until golden and rolls sound hollow when lightly tapped. Cool slightly to serve warm. Or, remove rolls from pan and cool on wire rack to serve later. Reheat if desired. Pull rolls apart to serve.

# New England Brown Bread

**Prep:** 15 minutes plus cooling ♦ **Bake:** 55 to 60 minutes
**Makes** 1 loaf, 12 servings

1. Preheat oven to 350°F. Grease 9" by 5" metal loaf pan. In large bowl, combine flours, raisins, sugar, baking soda, and salt. Stir in buttermilk, molasses, and egg until batter is just mixed (batter will be very wet).

2. Pour batter into loaf pan. Bake bread 55 to 60 minutes, until toothpick inserted in center of bread comes out clean.

3. With spatula, loosen bread from sides of pan. Remove bread from pan; cool slightly on wire rack to serve warm. Or, cool completely to serve later.

1 cup all-purpose flour
1 cup whole-wheat flour
¾ cup dark seedless raisins
¼ cup sugar
1¼ teaspoons baking soda
½ teaspoon salt
1¼ cups buttermilk or plain
    low-fat yogurt
¾ cup light molasses
1 large egg

**Each serving:** About
180 calories, 4 g protein,
41 g carbohydrate, 1 g total fat
(0 g saturated), 19 mg
cholesterol, 255 mg sodium.

◀ REFRIGERATOR
POTATO ROLLS AND
NEW ENGLAND
BROWN BREAD

♦

# *Desserts*

▲ ROASTED APPLES
WITH ICE CREAM P. 81

### Cake
¾ cup sugar
4 large eggs
1 cup all-purpose flour

### Coffee Syrup
1 cup (8 ounces) hot espresso or
   very strong brewed coffee
2 tablespoons sugar
3 tablespoons brandy

### Filling
1 container (16 to 17½ ounces)
   mascarpone cheese
½ cup milk
½ cup sugar
¾ cup heavy or whipping cream
4 squares (4 ounces) semisweet
   chocolate, grated
3 tablespoons unsweetened cocoa
   powder for dusting
Chocolate Curls for garnish
   (see following page), optional

**Each serving without chocolate
curls:** About 339 calories,
5 g protein, 31 g carbohydrate,
22 g total fat (14 g saturated)
94 mg cholesterol, 40 mg sodium.

## Tiramisu Cake

**Prep:** 30 minutes plus overnight to chill    ◆    **Bake:** 10 to 12 minutes
**Makes** 16 servings

1. *Prepare cake:* Preheat oven to 400°F. Grease three 8-inch round cake pans; line bottoms with waxed paper; grease paper. Dust pans with flour.

2. In large bowl, with mixer at low speed, beat sugar with eggs until blended. Increase speed to high; beat 5 to 10 minutes, until mixture is pale, thick, and creamy, and batter forms a thick ribbon when beaters are lifted. With rubber spatula, gently fold in flour until mixture is well-combined.

3. Pour batter into pans. Bake 8 to 10 minutes, until toothpick inserted in center of cake comes out clean. Cool in pans 1 minute; then invert onto wire rack to cool completely .

4. *Prepare coffee syrup:* In small bowl, stir together espresso, 2 tablespoons sugar, and brandy; let cool.

5. *Prepare filling:* In large bowl, with mixer at high speed, beat mascarpone, milk, and ½ cup sugar 3 minutes, or until very light and fluffy.

6. In small bowl, with same beaters, beat cream to soft peaks. With rubber spatula, gently fold whipped cream into mascarpone mixture.

7. Place 1 cake round, smooth side down, on cake plate. With pastry brush, brush one-third of coffee syrup over cake. Spread half the cheese filling, followed by half the grated chocolate. Continue layering the ingredients, ending with the third cake layer brushed with syrup. Cover and refrigerate overnight.

8. To serve, dust cake with cocoa and decorate with chocolate curls, if you like.

*T*IRAMISU CAKE ▶

*Chocolate Curls:* In 1-quart saucepan, heat 3 ounces (½ cup) semisweet chocolate pieces with 1 tablespoon vegetable shortening over low heat, stirring frequently, until melted and smooth. Pour chocolate mixture into foil-lined or disposable 5¾" by 3¼" loaf pan. Refrigerate about 2 hours, until chocolate is set. Remove chocolate from pan. Using a vegetable peeler, draw blade across surface of chocolate to make large curls. If chocolate appears too brittle to curl, let stand at room temperature 30 minutes to soften slightly. To avoid breaking curls, use a toothpick to lift and transfer to cake.

# Austrian Drum Torte

**Prep:** 2 hours 30 minutes plus chilling and cooling
**Bake:** 10 to 12 minutes per batch  ◆  **Makes** 16 servings

### Chocolate Ganache

1 package (8 ounces) semisweet chocolate squares, very finely chopped
1 bar (3 ounces) milk chocolate, very finely chopped
1 cup heavy or whipping cream
4 tablespoons butter or margarine, cut up

### Sponge Cake

12 large eggs, separated
1 cup sugar
2 teaspoons vanilla extract
1⅓ cups cake flour (not self-rising)
3 tablespoons butter or margarine, melted

### Caramel

⅓ cup sugar
1 tablespoon butter or margarine
1 teaspoon fresh lemon juice
2 tablespoons water
1 square (1 ounce) semisweet chocolate, melted

**Each serving:** About 360 calories, 7 g protein, 39 g carbohydrate, 20 g total fat (7 g saturated), 180 mg cholesterol, 145 mg sodium.

1. *Prepare chocolate ganache:* In medium bowl (preferably metal), combine semisweet and milk chocolates; set aside. In 2-quart saucepan, heat cream to boiling over medium-high heat. Pour over chocolate in bowl; let stand 1 minute. With rubber spatula, stir until mixture is smooth. Stir in butter until melted and smooth.

2. Place *2 inches cold water* and about *2 cups ice cubes* in very large bowl to make an ice bath. Set bowl with ganache in ice bath and chill, stirring ganache occasionally with rubber spatula, about 20 minutes, until mixture thickens and is an easy spreading consistency. (Or, chill uncovered in refrigerator at least 4 hours or overnight. Let come to room temperature; stir with spoon until an easy spreading consistency.)

3. *Prepare sponge cake:* Preheat oven to 400°F. Grease bottoms of two 9-inch round metal cake pans. Line each pan with a 9-inch reusable nonstick bakeware liner, or kitchen parchment, or waxed paper; grease parchment or waxed paper. (If using parchment or waxed paper, you will need to cut a total of seven 9-inch rounds. Liners are reusable and just need to be wiped clean.)

4. In small bowl, with mixer at high speed, beat egg yolks with ½ cup sugar about 10 minutes, until thick and lemon-colored. Beat in vanilla; set aside.

5. In large bowl, with clean beaters and with mixer at high speed, beat egg whites until soft peaks form. Beating at high speed, gradually sprinkle in remaining ½ cup sugar, 2 tablespoons at a time, beating well after each addition until sugar dissolves and whites stand in stiff peaks.

◀ 𝒜USTRIAN DRUM
TORTE

◆

(A) Carefully spread warm homemade caramel evenly over 1 cake
   layer with metal spatula.
(B) After caramel cools and layer is
   cut into 16 wedges, dip rounded
   edge of each wedge into melted
   semisweet chocolate.
(C) Arrange wedges on assembled
   cake, resting each on a ganache
   dollop at a 45-degree angle.

6. Transfer yolk mixture to very large bowl. Gradually sift in and fold flour
   into yolk mixture, then fold in melted butter until blended.

7. With spatula, fold beaten egg-white mixture into yolk mixture, one-
   third at a time, just until blended.

8. Spoon about 1 cup batter into each prepared pan. With metal spatula
   (preferably offset), gently spread batter to even thickness. Bake cake layers about 10 minutes, until lightly golden and cake springs back when
   gently touched with finger. Loosen edge of each layer with metal spatula; invert onto wire rack to cool completely. (If using liners, wipe clean
   before reusing. If using parchment or waxed paper, remove from layers
   after layers are cooled.)

9. When pans are cool, repeat with remaining batter to make 7 layers in
   all. Stack cooled cake layers between sheets of waxed paper.

10. *Prepare caramel:* In 1-quart saucepan, combine sugar, butter, lemon
    juice, and water and heat to boiling over high heat. Continue cooking,
    without stirring, about 4 minutes, until caramel is golden brown.

11. Carefully pour hot caramel over top of 1 cake layer; spread evenly with
    metal spatula (A). Cool caramel 2 minutes to set. With greased chef's

knife, cut layer in 16 wedges (do not let caramel cool too long; it will crack when it is cut). Dip rounded outside edge of each wedge into melted chocolate (B); place on waxed paper-lined cookie sheet to set.

12. *To assemble cake:* Spread ⅓ cup chocolate ganache on 1 cake layer. Top with second layer and spread with ⅓ cup ganache. Repeat 4 more times. Spoon remaining ganache into 16 dollops evenly spaced around edge of top layer. If serving within 2 hours, place 1 caramel-coated wedge, set at an angle, on top of each dollop (C). If not serving right away, refrigerate cake, but do not place wedges on top; the caramel will get soft in refrigerator.

13. To serve, remove cake from refrigerator at least 1 hour before serving, top with caramel wedges.

# Cream-Puff Wreath

**Prep:** 50 minutes plus chilling    ◆    **Bake:** 55 minutes
**Makes** 12 servings

## Pastry Cream
**3 large egg yolks**
**⅓ cup granulated sugar**
**3 tablespoons cornstarch**
**2 cups milk**
**2 teaspoons vanilla extract**

## Wreath
**6 tablespoons butter or margarine, cut up**
**1 cup water**
**1 cup all-purpose flour**
**4 large eggs**

## Almond Praline
**⅓ cup granulated sugar**
**¼ cup water**
**½ cup sliced natural almonds, toasted**
**1 cup heavy or whipping cream**
**1 tablespoon confectioners' sugar plus additional for garnish**

**Each serving:** About 295 calories, 7 g protein, 25 g carbohydrate, 19 g total fat (8 g saturated), 157 mg cholesterol, 125 mg sodium.

1. *Prepare pastry cream:* In medium bowl, with wire whisk, beat egg yolks, granulated sugar, and cornstarch until blended. In 3-quart saucepan, heat milk to simmering over medium-high heat. While constantly beating with wire whisk, gradually pour about half of simmering milk into yolk mixture. Return yolk mixture to saucepan and cook over low heat, whisking constantly, until mixture thickens and begins to bubble around edge of pan (mixture will not appear to boil vigorously); simmer 1 minute. Remove saucepan from heat; stir in vanilla. Transfer mixture to bowl. Cover surface directly with plastic wrap to prevent skin from forming and refrigerate at least 2 hours, until cold.

2. *Meanwhile prepare wreath:* Preheat oven to 425°F. Grease and flour large cookie sheet. Using 8-inch cake pan or plate as guide, trace circle in flour on cookie sheet with finger. Cut 1-inch opening from 1 corner of large zip-tight plastic bag.

3. In 2-quart saucepan, heat butter with water over high heat until butter melts and mixture boils. Reduce heat; add flour all at once and stir vigorously with wooden spoon until mixture forms ball and leaves side of saucepan. Remove from heat. Add eggs, 1 at a time, beating well with wooden spoon after each addition, until batter is smooth and satiny.

4. Spoon dough into plastic bag; squeeze down to corner with opening.

Using traced circle as guide, pipe dough in 1-inch-thick ring just inside circle on cookie sheet. Pipe another 1-inch-thick ring outside of first, making sure both are touching. With remaining dough, pipe a final ring on top along center seam of first 2 rings. With moistened finger, gently smooth dough rings where ends meet.

5. Bake wreath 20 minutes. Turn oven control to 375°F and bake 25 minutes longer, or until golden. Remove wreath from oven; poke side in several places with toothpick and bake 10 minutes longer. Transfer wreath to wire rack and cool completely.

6. *While wreath is cooling, prepare almond praline:* Lightly grease cookie sheet. In 1-quart saucepan, heat granulated sugar and water to boiling over high heat, swirling pan occasionally to help dissolve sugar. Boil mixture, without stirring, 5 to 7 minutes, until golden. Remove pan from heat and stir in ⅓ cup almonds; reserve remaining almonds for garnish. Stir mixture over low heat just until it liquefies. Immediately pour praline mixture onto cookie sheet; spread with back of spoon to ½-inch thickness. Let praline cool on cookie sheet on wire rack 10 minutes, or until firm.

▼ *C*REAM-PUFF WREATH

◆

7. Break praline into small pieces. In food processor with knife blade attached, process praline until ground into a fine powder.

8. *Assemble wreath:* With long serrated knife, slice wreath horizontally in half. If you like, pull out some of the moist interior of wreath and discard. In small bowl, with mixer at medium speed, beat cream and 1 tablespoon confectioners' sugar until stiff peaks form. Gently fold praline into chilled pastry cream; spoon into bottom of wreath. Top with whipped cream. Replace top of wreath. Refrigerate dessert if not serving right away.

9. To serve, sprinkle with confectioners' sugar; garnish with reserved almonds.

# Strawberry Dacquoise

1 cup pecans, toasted
2 tablespoons cornstarch
1½ cups plus 3 tablespoons
  confectioners' sugar
6 large egg whites
½ teaspoon cream of tartar
1 package (10 ounces) frozen
  quick-thaw strawberries
  in light syrup, thawed
1 envelope unflavored gelatin
2 cups heavy or whipping cream
1 pint strawberries

**Each serving:** About 305 calories, 4 g protein, 28 g carbohydrate, 21 g total fat (10 g saturated), 54 mg cholesterol, 45 mg sodium.

**Prep:** 1 hour plus chilling
**Bake:** 1 hour plus 1 hour 15 minutes to dry in oven  ◆  **Makes** 12 servings

1. In food processor with knife blade attached, or in blender at medium speed, process pecans, cornstarch, and ¾ cup confectioners' sugar until pecans are finely ground.

2. Line large cookie sheet with foil. With toothpick, outline three 13" by 4" rectangles on foil. Spray with nonstick cooking spray. Preheat oven to 275°F.

3. In large bowl, with mixer at high speed, beat egg whites and cream of tartar to soft peaks. Sprinkle in ¾ cup confectioners' sugar, 2 tablespoons at a time, beating well after each addition until sugar completely dissolves and whites stand in stiff, glossy peaks.

4. With rubber spatula, carefully fold ground pecan mixture into egg-white mixture. With metal spatula, spread one-third of meringue inside each rectangle on cookie sheet. Bake meringues 1 hour. Turn oven off; leave meringues in oven 1 hour 15 minutes to dry.

5. Cool meringues on cookie sheet on wire rack 10 minutes. Peel foil from meringues and cool completely. Store in airtight container at room temperature (to prevent sogginess) until ready to assemble.

6. In 2-quart saucepan, mash quick-thaw strawberries with their syrup. Sprinkle gelatin evenly over crushed strawberries; let stand 5 minutes to soften gelatin. Place saucepan over medium heat and cook strawberry mixture, stirring constantly, 2 to 3 minutes, until gelatin dissolves completely. Pour mixture into small bowl; chill over bowl of ice, stirring

▸ STRAWBERRY
DACQUOISE AND
OVEN-STEAMED
FIGGY PUDDING
◆

occasionally, about 15 minutes, until mixture thickens slightly to the consistency of egg whites.

7. In small bowl, with mixer at medium speed, beat heavy or whipping
cream and remaining 3 tablespoons confectioners' sugar until stiff peaks
form. Gently fold in thickened strawberry mixture.

8. On serving plate, place 1 meringue layer; spread with one-third of straw-
berry-cream filling. Repeat with remaining meringue layers and strawberry
filling, ending with strawberry filling. Cover dacquoise with plastic wrap
and refrigerate 4 hours to soften meringue layers for easier cutting.

9. To serve, hull strawberries. Cut one-third of strawberries in half; slice
remaining berries. Arrange halved and sliced berries on top of dacquoise.
Dust with confectioners' sugar, if you like.

# Oven-Steamed Figgy Pudding

2 packages (8 ounces each)
   dried Calimyrna figs
1¾ cups milk
1½ cups all-purpose flour
1 cup sugar
2½ teaspoons baking powder
1 teaspoon ground nutmeg
1 teaspoon ground cinnamon
1 teaspoon salt
3 large eggs
½ cup butter or margarine
   (1 stick), melted and
   cooled slightly
1½ cups fresh bread crumbs
   (from 3 to 4 slices white bread)
2 teaspoons grated orange peel
1 teaspoon grated lemon peel
marzipan fruit and greens
   for garnish
Brandied Hard Sauce (see below),
   optional

**Each serving without hard sauce:** About 350 calories, 6 g protein, 59 g carbohydrate, 11 g total fat (3 g saturated), 58 mg cholesterol, 430 mg sodium.

**Each tablespoon:** About 105 calories, 0 g protein, 11 g carbohydrate, 6 g total fat (1 g saturated), 0 mg cholesterol, 75 mg sodium.

**Prep:** 45 minutes ♦ **Bake:** 2 hours
**Makes** 12 servings

1. Preheat oven to 350°F. Grease 2½-quart metal steamed-pudding mold or fluted tube pan.
2. With kitchen shears, cut stems from figs; cut figs into small pieces. In 2-quart saucepan, combine figs and milk; cover and cook over medium-low heat, stirring occasionally, 10 to 15 minutes (mixture may look curdled). Be careful not to let mixture boil.
3. Meanwhile, in medium bowl, mix flour, sugar, baking powder, nutmeg, cinnamon, and salt.
4. In large bowl, with mixer at high speed, beat eggs 1 minute. Reduce speed to low; add butter, bread crumbs, orange peel, lemon peel, and fig mixture. Gradually add flour mixture; beat just until blended.
5. Spoon fig mixture into mold, smoothing top. Cover with sheet of greased foil, greased side down. (If your mold has a lid, grease the inside and do not use foil.) Place the mold in a deep roasting pan and place on oven rack. Pour hot tap *water* into roasting pan to come 2 inches up side of mold.
6. Bake pudding 2 hours or until firm and it pulls away from side of mold. Transfer pudding to wire rack; remove foil and cool 10 minutes. Invert onto serving plate; remove mold. Garnish with marzipan fruit and greens. Serve warm with brandied Hard Sauce, if you like.

*Brandied Hard Sauce:* In small bowl, with mixer at medium speed, beat 1½ cups confectioners' sugar, ½ cup butter or margarine (1 stick) softened, 2 tablespoons brandy, and ½ teaspoon vanilla extract until creamy. Refrigerate if not serving right away. Makes about 1 cup.

*Tip:* A delicious classic, Figgy Pudding was once an all-day activity of mixing ingredients, then steaming on the stovetop. Here, the ingredient list is lightened—we used butter instead of suet—and the cooking simplified—oven steaming is easy and foolproof. All the traditional flavor remains, but the preparation is streamlined for today's cook.

# Brandied Bûche de Noël

**Prep:** 1 hour 30 minutes plus cooling and chilling   ♦   **Bake:** 10 minutes
**Makes** 14 servings

1. *Prepare cake roll:* Preheat oven to 375°F. Grease 15½" by 10½" jelly-roll pan; line with waxed paper. Grease paper and dust with flour.

2. On sheet of waxed paper, combine flour, cocoa, cinnamon, ginger, cloves, and salt.

3. In small bowl, with mixer at high speed, beat egg whites and cream of tartar until soft peaks form. Beating at high speed, gradually sprinkle in ¼ cup granulated sugar, beating until sugar dissolves and whites stand in stiff peaks.

4. In large bowl, using same beaters and with mixer at high speed, beat egg yolks and remaining ¼ cup granulated sugar until very thick and lemon-colored.

5. With rubber spatula or wire whisk, gently fold beaten egg whites into beaten egg yolks, one-third at a time, then gently fold flour mixture into egg mixture, one-third at a time. Fold in melted butter, mixing just until combined.

6. With metal spatula, spread batter evenly in prepared pan. Bake 10 minutes, or until top of cake springs back when lightly touched with finger.

7. Sprinkle clean cloth towel with confectioners' sugar. When cake is done, immediately invert hot cake onto towel. Peel off waxed paper and discard.

## Cake

⅓ cup all-purpose flour
¼ cup unsweetened cocoa
1 teaspoon ground cinnamon
1 teaspoon ground ginger
pinch ground cloves
pinch salt
5 large eggs, separated
¼ teaspoon cream of tartar
½ cup granulated sugar
2 tablespoons butter or
    margarine, melted and
    cooled slightly
confectioners' sugar
nontoxic greens
Meringue Mushrooms
    (see following page)

## Brandied Butter Cream

1 cup granulated sugar
½ cup all-purpose flour
1 cup milk
1 square (1 ounce) unsweetened
    chocolate
1 square (1 ounce) semisweet
    chocolate
1 cup (2 sticks) butter or
    margarine, softened
2 tablespoons brandy
1 teaspoon vanilla extract

**Each serving:** About
310 calories, 4 g protein,
33 g carbohydrate, 19 g total fat
(4 g saturated), 78 mg cholesterol,
240 mg sodium.

◄ *B*RANDIED
BÛCHE DE NOËL

♦

Starting from a long side, roll cake with towel jelly-roll fashion. Cool cake roll, seam side down, on wire rack about 1 hour, until completely cool.

8. *Meanwhile, prepare brandied butter cream:* In 2-quart saucepan, combine granulated sugar and flour. With wire whisk, mix in milk until smooth. Cook over medium-high heat, stirring often, until mixture thickens and boils. Reduce heat and cook, stirring constantly, 2 minutes. Cool completely.

9. Meanwhile, in small saucepan, melt chocolates over low heat; cool slightly.

10. In large bowl, with mixer at medium speed, beat butter until creamy. Gradually beat in cooled flour mixture. When mixture is smooth, beat in brandy and vanilla extract until blended. Spoon half of white butter cream into small bowl; stir melted chocolate into butter cream remaining in large bowl.

11. *Assemble cake:* Gently unroll cooled cake. With metal spatula, spread white brandied butter cream almost to edges. Starting from a long side, roll cake without towel. With sharp knife, cut 1½-inch-thick diagonal slice off each end of roll; set aside. Place rolled cake, seam side down, on long platter. Spread some chocolate brandied butter cream over roll. Place 1 end piece on side of roll to resemble branch. Place remaining end piece on top of roll to resemble another branch. Spread remaining butter cream over roll and branches, leaving cut side of branches unfrosted. With metal spatula, spread frosting to resemble bark of tree. Refrigerate cake at least 2 hours before serving. Garnish platter with greens and meringue mushrooms.

# Meringue Mushrooms

2 large egg whites
⅛ teaspoon cream of tartar
⅓ cup sugar
unsweetened cocoa (optional)
1 square (1 ounce) semisweet
   chocolate, melted

**Each mushroom:** About
30 calories, 1 g protein,
6 g carbohydrate, 0 g total fat,
0 mg cholesterol, 10 mg sodium.

**Prep:** 20 minutes plus cooling    ◆   **Cook:** 2 hours
**Makes** 15 mushrooms.

1. Line large cookie sheet with foil.
2. In small bowl, with mixer at high speed, beat egg whites and cream of tartar until soft peaks form; gradually beat in sugar, 2 tablespoons at a time, beating well after each addition, until sugar completely dissolves and whites stand in stiff, glossy peaks.
3. Preheat oven to 200°F. Spoon meringue into large decorating bag with large writing tip. Pipe meringue onto cookie sheet in 15 mounds, each

about 1½ inches in diameter, to resemble mushroom caps. If you like, place some cocoa in small, fine-meshed strainer; use to dust meringue mushroom caps. Pipe remaining meringue onto cookie sheet in 15 upright 1¼-inch lengths to resemble mushroom stems.

4. Bake meringues 1½ hours. Turn oven off; let meringues stand in oven 30 minutes longer to dry. Cool completely on cookie sheet on wire rack.

5. With tip of paring knife, cut a small hole in center of underside of 1 mushroom cap. Dip pointed end of mushroom stem in melted chocolate; attach stem to cap by inserting chocolate-dipped end into hole in underside of mushroom cap. Repeat with remaining caps and stems. Let chocolate dry, about 1 hour.

6. Store mushrooms in tightly covered container up to 1 week.

# Cranberry-Almond Tart

**Prep:** 40 minutes plus cooling  ◆  **Bake:** 1 hour
**Makes** 10 servings

¼ teaspoon salt
1 cup plus 3 tablespoons all-purpose flour
8 tablespoons butter or margarine (1 stick)
2 to 3 tablespoons cold water plus ⅓ cup water
½ cup almond paste (about 5 ounces)
1¼ cups sugar
2 large eggs
½ teaspoon grated orange peel
1 bag (12-ounces) cranberries (3 cups)
lemon-peel strips for garnish

**Each serving:** About 340 calories, 5 g protein, 48 g carbohydrate, 15 g total fat (2 g saturated), 43 mg cholesterol, 190 mg sodium.

1. In medium bowl, mix salt and 1 cup flour. With pastry blender or 2 knives used scissor-fashion, cut in 4 tablespoons cold butter until mixture resembles coarse crumbs. Add 2 to 3 tablespoons cold water, 1 tablespoon at a time, mixing lightly with fork after each addition until dough is just moist enough to hold together. Shape dough into a disk; wrap with plastic wrap and freeze until firm enough to roll, about 15 minutes.

2. Meanwhile, in food processor with knife blade attached, blend almond paste, ½ cup sugar, and remaining 4 tablespoons softened butter until smooth. Add eggs and remaining 3 tablespoons flour; blend until well combined.

3. Preheat oven to 425°F. On lightly floured surface, with floured rolling pin, roll dough into 12-inch round. Press dough onto bottom and up side of 10" by 1" round tart pan with removable bottom. Fold overhang in and press against side of tart pan to form a thicker edge. With fork, prick dough all over to prevent puffing and shrinking during baking. Freeze 10 minutes, or until dough is firm.

4. Line tart shell with foil and fill with pie weights, dried beans, or uncooked rice. Bake tart shell 15 minutes, remove foil with weights and bake 10 minutes longer, or until golden. (If crust puffs up during baking, gently press it to tart pan with back of spoon.) Turn oven control to 350°F.

### CRANBERRY-ALMOND TART

◆

5. Fill hot tart shell with almond filling. Bake 20 to 25 minutes longer, until almond filling is slightly puffed and golden. Cool in pan on wire rack.

6. While tart shell is baking, in 2-quart saucepan, combine orange peel, 1 cup cranberries, remaining ¾ cup sugar, and ⅓ cup water and heat to boiling over high heat. Reduce heat to medium-low; simmer 5 minutes, or until mixture thickens slightly and cranberries pop. Stir in remaining 2 cups cranberries. Set aside until cool.

7. Remove almond-filled shell from pan; place on cake plate. Spoon cranberry topping over almond filling. Garnish with lemon-peel strips.

*Tip:* If you're pressed for time, make tart dough in a food processor. Using the knife blade, process flour, salt, shortening, and butter for 1 to 2 seconds. When mixture resembles fine crumbs, add an amount of ice water smaller than that called for in the recipe and process 1 to 2 seconds more, until dough begins to leave sides of bowl. Remove dough from bowl and shape into a ball.

# Praline-Iced Brownies

**Prep:** 20 minutes plus cooling ◆ **Bake:** 35 minutes
**Makes** 64 brownies

1. Preheat oven to 350°F. Line 13" by 9" metal baking pan with foil; grease foil.
2. In 3-quart saucepan, melt butter and chocolates over low heat, stirring frequently. Remove saucepan from heat. With wire whisk, beat in granulated sugar, then eggs, until well blended. Stir in vanilla, salt, then flour until blended. Spread batter evenly in pan.
3. Bake 35 minutes (toothpick inserted in brownies will not come out clean). Cool in pan on wire rack. If not using within 1 day, cover cooled brownies with foil and refrigerate or freeze for longer storage.
4. *Prepare praline topping:* In 2-quart saucepan, heat butter with brown sugar over medium-low heat, about 5 minutes, until mixture melts and bubbles. Remove saucepan from heat. With wire whisk, beat in bourbon or vanilla extract and water, then beat in confectioners' sugar until mixture is smooth.
5. With metal spatula, spread topping over room-temperature brownies; sprinkle with pecans. Cut brownies lengthwise into 8 strips, then cut each strip crosswise into 8 pieces.

### Brownies
1 cup butter or margarine
   (2 sticks)
4 squares (4 ounces) unsweetened
   chocolate
4 squares (4 ounces) semisweet
   chocolate
2¼ cups granulated sugar
6 large eggs
2 teaspoons vanilla extract
½ teaspoon salt
1¼ cups all-purpose flour

### Praline Topping
5 tablespoons butter or margarine
⅓ cup packed light brown sugar
3 tablespoons bourbon or
   1 tablespoon vanilla extract
2 tablespoons water
2 cups confectioners' sugar
½ cup pecans, toasted and
   coarsely chopped

**Each iced brownie:**
About 120 calories, 1 g protein,
16 g carbohydrate, 6 g total fat
(1 g saturated), 20 mg cholesterol,
75 mg sodium.

◀ *P*RALINE-ICED
BROWNIES AND
AMBROSIA LAYER
CAKE

◆

# Ambrosia Layer Cake

**Prep:** 1 hour 30 minutes plus cooling    &#9670;    **Bake:** 35 to 40 minutes
**Makes** 20 servings

### Orange Filling

4 large oranges
1 lemon
1 cup sugar
3 tablespoons cornstarch
½ cup butter or margarine (1 stick)
6 large egg yolks

### Cake

2½ cups cake flour (not self-rising)
1½ teaspoons baking powder
1 teaspoon baking soda
¼ teaspoon salt
1½ cups sugar
¾ cup butter or margarine (1½ sticks), softened
2 teaspoons vanilla extract
3 large eggs
1 cup buttermilk
1 cup flaked coconut
orange-peel curls for garnish

### Fluffy White Frosting

2 large egg whites
1 cup sugar
¼ cup water
2 teaspoons lemon juice
1 teaspoon light corn syrup
¼ teaspoon cream of tartar

**Each serving:** About 355 calories, 4 g protein, 52 g carbohydrate, 15 g total fat (4 g saturated), 96 mg cholesterol, 300 mg sodium.

1. *Prepare orange filling:* From oranges, grate 1 tablespoon peel and squeeze 1⅓ cups juice. From lemon, squeeze 1 tablespoon juice. In 3-quart saucepan, combine orange peel, orange juice, lemon juice, sugar, and cornstarch and stir until blended. Add butter and heat to boiling over medium heat; boil 1 minute.

2. In small bowl, beat yolks slightly. Into yolks, beat a small amount of orange mixture; pour egg mixture into orange mixture in saucepan. Reduce heat to low; cook, stirring constantly, 3 minutes, or until mixture is very thick. Pour into medium bowl; cover surface with plastic wrap to prevent skin from forming. Refrigerate until cold, about 2 hours.

3. *Prepare cake:* Preheat oven to 350°F. Grease and flour 13" by 9" metal baking pan. In medium bowl, combine flour, baking powder, baking soda, and salt; set aside.

4. In large bowl, with mixer at low speed, beat sugar and butter just until blended. Increase speed to high; beat until light and fluffy, 5 minutes, scraping bowl often with rubber spatula. Reduce speed to low; add vanilla extract and eggs, 1 at a time, and continue beating until blended. Alternately add flour mixture and buttermilk, ending with flour, and beat, occasionally scraping bowl, until batter is well mixed.

5. Spread batter in pan. Bake 35 to 40 minutes, until toothpick inserted in center of cake comes out clean. Cool in pan on wire rack 10 minutes. Invert cake onto wire rack to cool completely.

6. *Prepare fluffy white frosting:* In top of double boiler, over simmering water, with handheld mixer at high speed, beat egg whites, sugar, water, lemon juice, corn syrup, and cream of tartar, about 7 to 10 minutes, until soft peaks form. Remove double-boiler top from bottom; continue beating at high speed, about 7 to 10 minutes, until stiff peaks form.

7. *Assemble cake:* With serrated knife, cut cake horizontally in half. To remove top cake layer, carefully place cookie sheet in between cut layers and lift off top layer. With metal spatula, spread cooled orange filling on bottom layer. Transfer top layer of cake onto bottom layer by gently sliding cake onto filling.

8. Frost top and side of cake with fluffy white frosting. Sprinkle with coconut. Garnish with orange-peel curls.

# Roasted Apples with Ice Cream

**Prep:** 15 minutes    ◆    **Roast:** about 20 minutes
**Makes** 6 servings

1. Preheat oven to 425°F.
2. In 2-quart saucepan, melt butter over medium heat. Add sugar, raisins, lemon juice, and Calvados and cook, stirring constantly, until sugar melts.
3. Pour sugar mixture into 15½" by 10½" jelly-roll pan; add apples, cut sides down. Roast 20 minutes, without turning, or until apples are very soft.
4. Serve warm apples and their syrup with ice cream.

▲ ℛOASTED APPLES
WITH ICE CREAM

◆

4 tablespoons butter or margarine
¾ cup packed light brown sugar
⅓ cup golden raisins
2 tablespoons fresh lemon juice
2 tablespoons Calvados (apple brandy), apple juice, or water
6 small Granny Smith apples (about 1½ pounds), each cut in half and cored
1½ pints vanilla ice cream

**Each serving:** About 425 calories, 3 g protein, 66 g carbohydrate, 18 g total fat (7 g saturated), 4 g fiber, 35 mg cholesterol, 145 mg sodium.

# Lemon Bars

1½ cups plus 3 tablespoons
    all-purpose flour
½ cup plus 1 tablespoon
    confectioners' sugar
¾ cup cold butter or margarine
    (1½ sticks), cut into small
    pieces
2 large lemons
3 large eggs
1 cup granulated sugar
½ teaspoon baking powder
½ teaspoon salt

Each piece: About 95 calories,
1 g protein, 12 g carbohydrate,
4 g total fat (3 g saturated),
0 g fiber, 28 mg cholesterol,
85 mg sodium.

**Prep:** 15 minutes　◆　**Bake:** about 30 minutes
**Makes** 3 dozen pieces

1. Preheat oven to 350°F. Line 13" by 9" metal baking pan with foil, extending foil over short ends; lightly grease foil.
2. In medium bowl, combine 1½ cups flour and ½ cup confectioners' sugar. With pastry blender or 2 knives used scissor-fashion, cut in butter until mixture resembles coarse crumbs.
3. Sprinkle dough evenly into prepared pan. With floured hand, pat dough firmly into bottom. Bake 15 to 17 minutes, until lightly browned.
4. Meanwhile, from lemons, grate 1 teaspoon peel and squeeze ⅓ cup juice. In large bowl, with mixer at high speed, beat eggs until thick and lemon-colored, about 3 minutes. Reduce speed to low; add lemon peel and juice, granulated sugar, baking powder, salt, and remaining 3 tablespoons flour and beat until blended, scraping bowl occasionally.
5. Pour lemon filling over warm crust. Bake 15 minutes, or until filling is just set and golden around edges. Transfer pan to wire rack. Sift remaining 1 tablespoon confectioners' sugar over warm filling. Cool completely in pan on wire rack.
6. When cool, transfer with foil to cutting board. Cut into diamonds or bars.

# *Beverages*

## Holiday Eggnog

**Prep:** 10 minutes plus chilling  ♦  **Cook:** 25 minutes
**Makes** about 16 cups or 32 servings

1. In heavy 4-quart saucepan, with wire whisk, beat eggs, sugar, and salt until blended. Gradually stir in 1 quart milk and cook over low heat, stirring constantly, until custard thickens and coats the back of a spoon well, about 25 minutes (mixture should be about 160°F, but do not boil or it will curdle).
2. Pour custard into large bowl; stir in rum, if using, vanilla extract, 1 teaspoon ground nutmeg, and remaining 1 quart milk. Cover and refrigerate until well chilled, at least 3 hours.
3. In small bowl, with mixer at medium speed, beat heavy or whipping cream until soft peaks form. With wire whisk, gently fold whipped cream into custard mixture.
4. To serve, pour eggnog into chilled 5-quart punch bowl; sprinkle with nutmeg for garnish.

12 large eggs
1¼ cups sugar
½ teaspoon salt
2 quarts whole milk
1 cup dark rum (optional)
2 tablespoons vanilla extract
1 teaspoon ground nutmeg plus additional for sprinkling
1 cup heavy or whipping cream

**Each serving:** About 125 calories, 5 g protein, 11 g carbohydrate, 7 g total fat (4 g saturated), 0 g fiber, 98 mg cholesterol, 90 mg sodium.

2 cups sugar

1 medium orange, thinly sliced

1 small lemon, thinly sliced

3 cinnamon sticks (3 inches each)

8 whole cloves

1 bottle (750 milliliters)
  dry red wine

1 small orange, studded with
  cloves and thinly sliced

**Each serving wine:** About
130 calories, 0 g protein,
27 g carbohydrate, 0 g total fat,
0 g fiber, 0 mg cholesterol,
5 mg sodium.

**Each serving cider:** About
140 calories, 0 g protein,
36 g carbohydrate, 0 g total fat,
0 g fiber, 0 mg cholesterol,
5 mg sodium.

Whipped Cream

1 cup heavy or whipping cream

2 tablespoons confectioners' sugar

2 teaspoons vanilla extract

Hot Chocolate

6 ounces semisweet chocolate,
  chopped

1½ cups whole milk

unsweetened cocoa for sprinkling
  (optional)

**Each serving:** About 165 calories,
2 g protein, 11 g carbohydrate,
13 g total fat (8 g saturated),
1 g fiber, 32 mg cholesterol,
25 mg sodium.

# Hot Mulled Wine

**Prep:** 10 minutes   ◆   **Cook:** 20 minutes
**Makes** about 8 cups or 16 servings

1. In nonreactive 4-quart saucepan, combine sugar, orange slices, lemon slices, cinnamon sticks, cloves, and 1 cup water; heat to boiling over high heat, stirring until sugar dissolves. Reduce heat to medium and cook 3 minutes.
2. Add wine to saucepan and heat, stirring, until hot (do not boil). Add clove-studded orange slices. Serve hot.

*Hot Mulled Cider:* Prepare Hot Mulled Wine as above except delete water and use 2 tablespoons brown sugar in place of 2 cups granulated sugar. Add ½ gallon apple cider in step 1 and delete wine in step 2.

# Hot Chocolate

**Prep:** 10 minutes   ◆   **Cook:** 10 minutes
**Makes** about 4 cups or 12 servings

1. *Prepare whipped cream:* In small bowl, with mixer at medium speed, beat cream with sugar and vanilla until stiff peaks form. Cover and refrigerate if not using right away.
2. *Prepare hot chocolate:* Place chocolate in 1-quart saucepan. Pour ⅓ cup boiling water over chocolate and stir until chocolate melts. Add milk and 1⅓ cups boiling water; heat over medium heat until hot but not boiling, whisking constantly. Serve with a dollop of cream. Sprinkle with cocoa, if you like.

# Light Eggnog

**Prep:** 15 minutes plus chilling   ◆   **Cook:** 15 minutes

**Makes** about 13 cups or 26 servings

6 large eggs
6 large egg whites
2 quarts whole milk
1¼ cups sugar
¼ cup cornstarch
½ teaspoon salt
1 cup dark rum (optional)
2 tablespoons vanilla extract
1 teaspoon ground nutmeg plus
   additional for sprinkling

1. In large bowl, with wire whisk, beat eggs and egg whites until blended. In heavy 3-quart saucepan, with clean wire whisk, mix 1 quart milk, sugar, cornstarch, and salt until blended. Heat to boiling over medium-high heat, stirring constantly, until mixture has thickened slightly; boil 1 minute. Gradually whisk about 1 cup simmering milk into egg mixture; pour egg mixture back into milk, whisking constantly.
2. With wooden spoon, stir mixture constantly until thermometer reaches 160°F, about 3 minutes. (Do not boil or it will curdle.) Pour custard into large bowl; stir in remaining 1 quart milk, rum, if using, vanilla, and 1 teaspoon nutmeg. Cover and refrigerate until well chilled, at least 3 hours or up to 1 day.
3. Pour eggnog into chilled 5-quart punch bowl; sprinkle with nutmeg.

**Each serving:** About 110 calories, 5 g protein, 15 g carbohydrate, 4 g total fat (2 g saturated), 0 g fiber, 60 mg cholesterol, 100 mg sodium.

# Wassail

**Prep:** 10 minutes   ◆   **Cook:** 25 minutes

**Makes** about 8 cups or 16 servings

½ gallon apple cider or juice
1 lemon, thinly sliced
2 tablespoons brown sugar
2 cinnamon sticks (3 inches each)
12 whole allspice
12 whole cloves
6 lady apples or 1 Golden
   Delicious apple
1 cup applejack or apple brandy

1. In 5-quart Dutch oven, combine cider, lemon slices, brown sugar, cinnamon sticks, and allspice; heat to boiling over medium-high heat. Reduce heat and simmer 10 minutes.
2. Insert 2 cloves into each lady apple or all cloves into Golden Delicious apple. Add apples and applejack to cider and cook until heated through, about 2 minutes.

**Each serving:** About 110 calories, 0 g protein, 18 g carbohydrate, 0 g total fat, 0 g fiber, 0 mg cholesterol, 5 mg sodium.

▲ MARINATED
OLIVES P. 88

# Gifts from the Kitchen

## Candied Citrus Peel

3 large grapefruit or
  5 navel oranges
3½ cups sugar
1½ cups water

**Each ounce:** About 95 calories,
0 g protein, 24 g carbohydrate,
0 g fat, 0 mg cholesterol, 0 mg
sodium.

𝒞ANDIED ▶
**CITRUS PEEL**

◆

**Prep:** 20 minutes plus cooling and drying
**Cook:** about 1 hour 30 minutes   ◆   **Makes** about 2 pounds

1. Score peel of each fruit into quarters, cutting just through the rind and white pith. Pull peel from fruit (you should have about 14 ounces peel). Refrigerate fruit for another use. Cut grapefruit peel crosswise or orange peel lengthwise into strips about ¼ inch wide.

2. In 4-quart saucepan, combine peel and enough *water* to cover; heat to boiling over high heat. Boil 5 minutes; drain.

3. Repeat step 2, two more times, draining peel well and using fresh water each time (3 blanchings in all).

4. In 12-inch skillet, combine 2½ cups sugar with 1½ cups water; cook over high heat, stirring constantly, until sugar dissolves and mixture boils. Boil, stirring occasionally, 15 minutes. (If using a candy thermometer, temperature should read 230° to 235°F.)

5. Add drained peel to syrup in skillet and stir to coat evenly. Reduce heat and simmer, partially covered, 1 hour, or until peel has absorbed most of syrup, stirring occasionally. Remove cover and continue to simmer, stirring gently, until all syrup has been absorbed.

6. On sheet of waxed paper, place remaining 1 cup sugar. With tongs, lightly roll peel, a few pieces at a time, in sugar; place in single layer on wire racks. Let peel dry at least 12 hours or overnight. Dry longer if necessary; peels should be dry on the outside but still moist on the inside. Store at room temperature in airtight container up to 1 month.

# Marinated Olives

¼ cup extravirgin olive oil

2 teaspoons fennel seeds, crushed

4 small bay leaves

2 pounds assorted Mediterranean olives (such as niçoise, picholine, Kalamata, and oil-cured)

6 strips (3" by 1" each) lemon peel

4 garlic cloves, crushed with side of chef's knife

**Each ¼ cup:** About 90 calories, 0 g protein, 3 g carbohydrate, 10 g total fat (1 g saturated), 0 mg cholesterol, 700 mg sodium.

**Prep:** 10 minutes plus chilling   ◆   **Chill:** 24 hours
**Makes** about 6 cups

1. In 1-quart saucepan, heat oil, fennel seeds, and bay leaves over medium heat until hot but not smoking. Remove saucepan from heat; let stand 10 minutes.
2. In large bowl, combine olive-oil mixture with olives, lemon peel, and garlic. Cover bowl and refrigerate olives at least 24 hours to allow flavors to develop, stirring occasionally. (Or, in large zip-tight plastic bag, combine all ingredients, turning to coat olives well. Seal bag, pressing out as much air as possible. Place on plate; refrigerate, turning bag occasionally.)
3. Spoon olives into jars for gift giving. Store in refrigerator up to 1 month.

*A*RRABBIATA ▶
SAUCE,
ROSEMARY-FENNEL
BREADSTICKS,
AND MARINATED
OLIVES

◆

# Arrabbiata Sauce

**Prep:** 15 minutes ◆ **Cook:** about 1 hour ◆ **Makes** about 14 cups

1. In 8-quart Dutch oven, heat oil over medium heat until hot but not smoking. Add garlic and cook, stirring, 2 minutes; do not brown. Stir in tomatoes with their juice, salt, and red pepper; heat to boiling over high heat. Reduce heat; simmer, uncovered, 50 minutes, or until sauce thickens slightly, stirring occasionally and crushing tomatoes with side of spoon.
2. For smooth, traditional texture, press tomato mixture through food mill into large bowl. Or, leave sauce as is for a hearty, chunky texture. Cool sauce slightly. Spoon into jars. Store in refrigerator up to 1 week; or spoon into freezer-proof containers and freeze up to 2 months.

*Tip:* It's never too early to start collecting containers for all the goodies you'll give away at Christmas. Save jars with interesting shapes and in all sizes and spray their tops with gold or silver paint. Line unusual baskets with fabric printed with seasonal motifs, or thread bright-colored ribbons through open-weave baskets. Browse through summer flea markets for vintage cookie tins.

½ cup extravirgin olive oil
6 garlic cloves, crushed with side of chef's knife
4 cans (35 ounces each) Italian plum tomatoes
1 tablespoon salt
1 to 1½ teaspoons crushed red pepper

**Each ¼ cup:** About 30 calories, 1 g protein, 3 g carbohydrate, 2 g total fat (0 g saturated), 0 mg cholesterol, 230 mg sodium.

# Rosemary-Fennel Breadsticks

**Prep:** 40 minutes ◆ **Bake:** 20 minutes per batch
**Makes** 64 breadsticks

1. In large bowl, combine yeast, salt, fennel seeds, rosemary, pepper, and 2 cups flour. With spoon, stir in warm water; beat vigorously with spoon 1 minute. Stir in oil. Gradually stir in 2¼ cups flour.
2. Turn dough onto floured surface and knead until smooth and elastic, about 8 minutes, working in more flour (about ½ cup) while kneading. Cover dough loosely with plastic wrap; let rest 10 minutes.
3. Preheat oven to 375°F. Grease 2 large cookie sheets. Divide dough in half. Keeping one-half of dough covered, cut other half into 32 pieces. Shape each piece into 12-inch-long rope. Place ropes, about 1 inch apart, on cookie sheets.
4. Place cookie sheets on 2 oven racks and bake breadsticks 20 minutes, or until golden and crisp throughout, rotating cookie sheets between upper and lower racks halfway through baking time. Transfer breadsticks to wire racks to cool. Repeat with remaining dough.

2 packages quick-rise yeast
2½ teaspoons salt
2 teaspoons fennel seeds, crushed
1 teaspoon dried rosemary, crumbled
½ teaspoon coarsely ground black pepper
about 4¾ cups all-purpose flour
1⅓ cups very warm water (120° to 130°F)
½ cup olive oil

**Each breadstick:** About 50 calories, 1 g protein, 7 g carbohydrate, 2 g total fat (0 g saturated), 0 mg cholesterol, 85 mg sodium.

# Hot and Sweet Nut Brittle

1 pound blanched whole almonds
¼ cup cider vinegar
2 cups plus 1 tablespoon sugar
2 teaspoons salt
2 teaspoons ground cumin
1 teaspoon ground coriander
½ to ¾ teaspoon ground
    red pepper (cayenne)

Each ounce: About 145 calories,
4 g protein, 18 g carbohydrate,
8 g total fat (1 g saturated),
0 mg cholesterol, 155 mg
sodium.

**Prep:** 20 minutes    ◆    **Cook:** about 30 minutes
**Makes** about 1¾ pounds

1. Preheat oven to 375°F. Place almonds in 15½" by 10½" jelly-roll pan. Bake, shaking pan occasionally, 10 to 15 minutes, until golden brown. Cool almonds in pan on wire rack.
2. While almonds cool, in heavy 3-quart saucepan, heat vinegar and 2 cups sugar to boiling over medium heat. Continue cooking over medium heat, stirring occasionally, 15 to 20 minutes, until mixture turns dark amber in color. (If using a candy thermometer, temperature should read about 360°F.)
3. Meanwhile, in small bowl, mix salt, cumin, coriander, ground red pepper, and remaining 1 tablespoon sugar. Lightly grease large cookie sheet.
4. Remove saucepan from heat. Stir spice mixture into hot sugar syrup. Add almonds and stir until evenly coated. Immediately pour mixture onto cookie sheet. With 2 forks, spread almond mixture to form a single layer.
5. Cool brittle completely on cookie sheet on wire rack. With hands, break brittle into small pieces. Store in tightly covered jar or tin up to 1 month.

# Chocolate Truffles

8 ounces bittersweet chocolate
½ cup heavy or whipping cream
3 tablespoons unsalted butter,
    softened and cut up (do not
    use margarine)
⅓ cup hazelnuts (filberts),
    toasted and finely chopped
3 tablespoons unsweetened cocoa

Each truffle: About 65 calories,
1 g protein, 5 g carbohydrate,
6 g total fat (3 g saturated),
8 mg cholesterol, 2 mg sodium.

**Prep:** 25 minutes plus chilling
**Makes** 32 truffles

1. In food processor with knife blade attached, process chocolate until finely ground.
2. In 1-quart saucepan, heat heavy cream over medium-high heat to boiling. Add cream to chocolate in food processor and blend until smooth. Add butter and blend well.
3. Line 9" by 5" metal loaf pan with plastic wrap. Pour chocolate mixture into pan; spread evenly. Refrigerate about 3 hours, until cool and firm enough to handle.
4. Remove chocolate mixture from pan by lifting edges of plastic wrap and inverting chocolate block onto cutting board; discard plastic wrap. Cut chocolate block into 32 pieces. (To cut chocolate mixture easily, dip knife in hot water and wipe dry.) Quickly roll each piece into a ball. Roll half

of balls in chopped hazelnuts and roll other half of balls in cocoa. Refrigerate truffles in airtight containers up to 1 week or freeze up to 1 month. Remove from freezer 1 hour before serving.

# Butterscotch Sauce

**Prep:** 5 minutes ◆ **Cook:** 10 minutes
**Makes** about 6 cups

4 cups packed light brown sugar
2 cups heavy or whipping cream
1⅓ cups light corn syrup
½ cup butter or margarine (1 stick)
4 teaspoons distilled white vinegar
½ teaspoon salt
4 teaspoons vanilla extract

1. In 5-quart Dutch oven (do not use smaller pot because mixture bubbles up during cooking), combine brown sugar, heavy cream, corn syrup, butter, vinegar, and salt; heat to boiling over high heat, stirring occasionally. Reduce heat; simmer, uncovered, stirring frequently, 5 minutes.
2. Remove Dutch oven from heat; stir in vanilla. Sauce will have thin consistency when hot but will thicken when chilled. Cool sauce completely. Transfer to jars with tight-fitting lids. Store in refrigerator up to 2 weeks. Reheat to serve warm over ice cream.

**Each tablespoon:** About 75 calories, 0 g protein, 13 g carbohydrate, 3 g total fat (1 g saturated), 7 mg cholesterol, 35 mg sodium.

# Peanut Butter Cups

**Prep:** 40 minutes plus chilling
**Makes** 60 candies

9 ounces white chocolate or 1½ packages (6 ounces each) white baking bars, chopped
1½ cups creamy peanut butter
1 package (8 ounces) semisweet chocolate squares, chopped
⅓ cup lightly salted cocktail peanuts, chopped

**Each candy:** About 85 calories, 2 g protein, 7 g carbohydrate, 6 g total fat ( 2 g saturated), 1 mg cholesterol, 40 mg sodium.

1. Arrange 60 miniature (1" by ¼") paper or foil baking cups on 15½" by 10½" jelly-roll pan.
2. In heavy 2-quart saucepan, heat chopped white chocolate and ¼ cup peanut butter over low heat, stirring occasionally, until melted and smooth. Spoon peanut-butter mixture into baking cups. Refrigerate 10 minutes.
3. Meanwhile, in heavy 2-quart saucepan, heat chopped semisweet chocolate and remaining 1¼ cups peanut butter over low heat, stirring occasionally, until melted and smooth.
4. Spoon warm chocolate-peanut butter mixture over chilled mixture in baking cups; sprinkle with peanuts. Refrigerate overnight. Store candies, covered, in refrigerator up to 1 week or in airtight container in freezer up to 1 month.

# Old-Fashioned Fruit Cakes

2 cups dark seedless raisins

1 cup dried apricots, coarsely
  chopped

1 cup dried Calimyrna figs,
  coarsely chopped

1 cup pitted dates, coarsely
  chopped

1 cup brandy

2½ cups all-purpose flour

1 teaspoon baking powder

1 teaspoon salt

1 teaspoon ground cinnamon

½ teaspoon baking soda

½ teaspoon ground nutmeg

½ teaspoon ground allspice

1¼ cups packed light
  brown sugar

1 cup butter or margarine
  (2 sticks), softened

5 large eggs

¼ cup light molasses

1 teaspoon grated orange peel

2 cups coarsely chopped
  walnuts or pecans

**Each serving:** About
175 calories, 3 g protein,
25 g carbohydrate, 8 g total fat
(1 g saturated), 22 mg
cholesterol, 125 mg sodium.

**O**LD-FASHIONED ▶
FRUIT CAKE

◆

**Prep:** 40 minutes plus standing     ◆     **Bake:** 60 to 70 minutes
**Makes** 6 small (12-ounce) fruitcakes, each 8 servings

1. In large bowl, combine raisins, apricots, figs, dates, and ¾ cup brandy;
   toss to combine. Cover and let stand 4 hours or overnight.

2. Preheat oven to 300°F. Grease six 5¾" by 3¼" loaf pans; line bottoms
   with waxed paper; grease paper. Dust with flour. In medium bowl, combine flour, baking powder, salt, cinnamon, baking soda, nutmeg, and allspice; set aside.

3. In another large bowl, with mixer at low speed, beat brown sugar with butter until blended. Increase speed to high; beat until light and creamy. At low speed, add eggs, 1 at a time, beating well after each addition. Add molasses, orange peel, and flour mixture and beat until blended. With spoon, stir in dried-fruit mixture and nuts.

4. Spoon batter evenly into pans. On bottom oven rack, pour boiling water into roasting pan to fill halfway. Place fruitcakes on rack above. Bake fruitcakes 60 to 70 minutes, until tops are golden and toothpick inserted in center comes out clean with a few moist crumbs attached.

5. Cool fruitcakes in pans on wire rack 30 minutes. Remove from pans; discard waxed paper. Brush remaining ¼ cup brandy over tops of warm cakes. Cool completely. Wrap each fruitcake well with plastic wrap or foil. Store at room temperature up to 1 week or refrigerate up to 1 month.

# Pear Chutney

**Prep:** 30 minutes   ♦   **Cook:** about 15 minutes
**Makes** about 6 cups

12 ounces dried pear halves, chopped (2 cups)
1 large red onion, finely chopped (1 cup)
2½ cups pear nectar
2 cups dark seedless and/or golden raisins
¾ cup cider vinegar
½ cup dried tart cherries
⅓ cup sugar
1 tablespoon mustard seeds
1 tablespoon grated, peeled fresh ginger
¼ teaspoon salt
1 cinnamon stick (3 inches)
1 cup water

1. In 4-quart saucepan, combine all ingredients and heat to boiling over high heat, stirring occasionally. Reduce heat; simmer, uncovered, 15 minutes, or until pears are very soft, stirring frequently.

2. Discard cinnamon stick. Spoon chutney into jars; cover tightly. Store in refrigerator up to 1 month.

*Tip:* Your jars of delicious homemade sauces and preserves or baskets of scrumptious baked goodies deserve special attention when you wrap them for gifts. Enclose them in layers of colored cellophane or tulle sparkled with spray-on glitter. Use wide grosgrain, wired organza, or velvet ribbon for pretty bows—or go for the natural look with easy-to-handle raffia. Loop the bow around a cookie cutter, or a bundle of cinnamon sticks, or a spray of pepper berries for a touch of whimsy.

**Each ¼ cup:** About
115 calories, 1 g protein,
30 g carbohydrate, 0 g total fat,
0 mg cholesterol, 25 mg sodium.

1 cup butter (2 sticks), softened
   (do not use margarine)
1½ cups sugar
2 large eggs
1 teaspoon vanilla extract
3 cups all-purpose flour
½ teaspoon baking powder
½ teaspoon salt
Ornamental Frosting (see page
   96), optional

**Each cookie without frosting:**
About 60 calories, 1 g protein,
8 g carbohydrate, 3 g total fat
(2 g saturated), 13 mg cholesterol,
45 mg sodium.

*𝒢*REAT-GRANNY'S ▶
**OLD-TIME SPICE COOKIES,**
**SAND TARTS, AND**
**JELLY CENTERS**
*(clockwise from top of plate)*

◆

# *Cookies*

## Sand Tarts

**Prep:** 1 hour 30 minutes plus chilling, cooling, and decorating
**Bake:** 12 to 15 minutes per batch  •  **Makes** about 6 dozen cookies

1. In large bowl, with mixer at low speed, beat butter with sugar until blended. Increase speed to high; beat until light and creamy. At low speed, beat in eggs and vanilla until mixed, then beat in flour, baking powder, and salt, occasionally scraping bowl with rubber spatula, until well combined. Shape dough into 4 balls; flatten each slightly. Wrap each ball in plastic wrap and freeze at least 1 hour or refrigerate overnight, until dough is firm enough to roll.

2. Preheat oven to 350°F. On lightly floured surface, with floured rolling pin, roll out 1 piece of dough slightly thinner than ¼ inch, keeping remaining dough refrigerated. With floured 3- to 4-inch assorted cookie cutters, cut dough into as many cookies as possible; reserve trimmings. Place cookies, about 1 inch apart, on ungreased large cookie sheet.

3. Bake cookies 12 to 15 minutes, until golden around edges. With wide spatula, transfer cookies to wire rack to cool. Repeat with remaining dough and trimmings.

4. When cookies are cool, prepare Ornamental Frosting, if you like; use to decorate cookies as desired. Set cookies aside to allow frosting to dry completely, about 1 hour.

# Great-Granny's Old-Time Spice Cookies

5½ cups all-purpose flour
1 teaspoon ground cinnamon
1 teaspoon ground allspice
½ teaspoon ground nutmeg
½ teaspoon baking soda
½ teaspoon salt
1 cup butter or margarine
  (2 sticks), softened
1¼ cups packed light brown
  sugar
1 jar (12 ounces) dark molasses
Ornamental Frosting (see below),
  optional

**Each cookie without frosting:**
About 120 calories, 2 g protein,
21 g carbohydrate, 4 g total fat
(1 g saturated), 0 mg cholesterol,
95 mg sodium.

**Each tablespoon:** About
40 calories, 0 g protein,
10 g carbohydrate, 0 g total fat
(0 g saturated), 0 mg cholesterol,
3 mg sodium.

**Prep:** 1 hour 10 minutes plus chilling, cooling, and decorating
**Bake:** 8 to 10 minutes per batch    ◆    **Makes** about 4 dozen cookies

1. In large bowl, combine flour, cinnamon, allspice, nutmeg, baking soda, and salt. In another large bowl, with mixer at low speed, beat butter with brown sugar until blended. Increase speed to high; beat until light and creamy. At low speed, beat in molasses until blended, then beat in 3 cups flour mixture. With spoon, stir in remaining flour mixture. Divide dough into 4 equal pieces. Wrap each piece in plastic wrap and freeze at least 1 hour or refrigerate overnight, until dough is firm enough to roll.

2. Preheat oven to 350°F. On well-floured surface, with floured rolling pin, roll out 1 piece of dough ⅛ inch thick, keeping remaining dough refrigerated (dough will be soft). With floured 3-to 4-inch assorted cookie cutters, cut dough into as many cookies as possible; reserve trimmings. Place cookies, about 1 inch apart, on ungreased large cookie sheet.

3. Bake cookies 8 to 10 minutes, just until browned. Cool cookies on cookie sheet 5 minutes. With wide spatula, transfer cookies to wire rack to cool completely. Repeat with remaining dough and trimmings.

4. When cookies are cool, prepare Ornamental Frosting, if you like; use to decorate cookies as desired. Set cookies aside to allow frosting to dry completely, about 1 hour.

*Ornamental Frosting:* In bowl, with mixer at medium speed, beat 1 package (16 ounces) confectioners' sugar, 3 tablespoons meringue powder, and ⅓ cup warm water about 5 minutes, until blended and mixture is so stiff that knife drawn through it leaves a clean-cut path. If you like, tint frosting with food colorings or food-color pastes; keep covered with plastic wrap to prevent drying out. With small metal spatula, artist's paintbrushes, or decorating bags with small writing tips, decorate cookies with frosting. (You may need to thin frosting with a little warm water.) Makes about 3 cups.

# Jelly Centers

**Prep:** 45 minutes plus chilling and cooling
**Bake:** 10 to 12 minutes per batch
**Makes** about 4½ dozen sandwich cookies

1. In large bowl, with mixer at low speed, beat butter with 1 cup sugar, occasionally scraping bowl with rubber spatula, until blended. Increase speed to high; beat until light and fluffy. At low speed, beat in egg yolks and vanilla until blended. Gradually beat in flour, baking powder, and salt. Shape dough into 2 balls; flatten each slightly. Wrap each in plastic wrap; refrigerate 1 hour or until firm enough to roll.

2. Preheat oven to 350°F. Between 2 sheets of floured waxed paper, roll out half of dough ⅛ inch thick, keeping remaining dough refrigerated. With floured 2-inch cookie cutter, cut out as many cookies as possible. Place cookies, ½ inch apart, on ungreased large cookie sheet; reserve trimmings. With ½-inch round or star-shaped cookie cutter, cut out centers from half of cookies. Remove centers; add to trimmings.

3. In cup, beat egg whites slightly. Brush cookies with cut-out centers with some egg white, then sprinkle with some of remaining ¼ cup sugar. Bake all cookies 10 to 12 minutes, until cookies are lightly browned. Transfer cookies to wire rack to cool.

4. Repeat steps 2 and 3 with remaining dough and trimmings to make more cookies.

5. When cookies are cool, spread center of each cookie without cut-out center with ¼ to ½ teaspoon jam; top each with a cookie with a cut-out center, gently pressing cookies together to form a sandwich.

1 cup butter or margarine
  (2 sticks), softened
1¼ cups sugar
2 large eggs, separated
2 teaspoons vanilla extract
3 cups all-purpose flour
⅛ teaspoon baking powder
⅛ teaspoon salt
about 1 cup raspberry preserves

**Each sandwich cookie:** About 95 calories, 1 g protein, 14 g carbohydrate, 4 g total fat (1 g saturated), 8 mg cholesterol, 55 mg sodium.

▼ *AUNT TESS'S ANISETTE COOKIES, GOOD HOUSEKEEPING GINGERBREAD CUTOUTS, AND LAYERED DATE BARS* (from left)

◆

# Layered Date Bars

1 package (10 ounces) pitted dates
    (2 cups), coarsely chopped
½ cup walnuts, finely chopped
¼ cup sugar
1¼ cups water
1½ cups all-purpose flour
1½ cups old-fashioned oats,
    uncooked
1 cup packed brown sugar
1 teaspoon baking soda
¾ cup butter or margarine
    1½ sticks), softened

Each bar: About 155 calories,
2 g protein, 25 g carbohydrate,
6 g total fat (1 g saturated),
0 mg cholesterol, 100 mg sodium.

**Prep:** 30 minutes plus cooling  ◆  **Bake:** 40 minutes
**Makes** 32 bars

1. Preheat oven to 350°F. In 2-quart saucepan, combine dates, walnuts, sugar, and water and heat to boiling over high heat. Reduce heat; simmer, uncovered, stirring occasionally, 10 to 15 minutes, until dates are soft and mixture is thick. Set aside.
2. Meanwhile, in large bowl, combine flour, oats, brown sugar, and baking soda. With hand, knead in butter until dough forms. Press half of dough evenly in bottom of 13" by 9" metal baking pan. Bake 15 minutes, or until pale golden.
3. Spread date mixture evenly over hot crust. Sprinkle remaining oat mixture on top. Bake 25 minutes longer, or until golden. Cool completely in pan on wire rack. When cool, cut lengthwise into 4 strips, then cut each strip crosswise into 8 pieces.

# Aunt Tess's Anisette Cookies

½ cup butter or margarine
    (1 stick), softened
½ cup granulated sugar
3 large eggs
1 teaspoon vanilla extract
2 teaspoons anise extract or
    anisette
2½ cups all-purpose flour
1 tablespoon baking powder
¾ cup confectioners' sugar
2 tablespoons water
red and green sprinkles (optional)

Each cookie without sprinkles:
About 80 calories, 1 g protein,
12 g carbohydrate, 3 g total fat
(1 g saturated), 18 mg cholesterol,
70 mg sodium.

**Prep:** 1 hour plus chilling and cooling  ◆  **Bake:** 12 minutes per batch
**Makes** 3 dozen cookies

1. In large bowl, with mixer at low speed, beat butter with granulated sugar until blended. Increase speed to high; beat until creamy. At medium speed, beat in eggs, vanilla, and 1 teaspoon anise extract, constantly scraping bowl with rubber spatula. Reduce speed to low; beat in flour and baking powder, occasionally scraping bowl, until blended. Shape dough into 4 balls. Wrap each ball in plastic wrap and freeze at least 1 hour or refrigerate overnight.
2. Preheat oven to 350°F. On lightly floured surface, divide 1 ball of dough into 9 equal pieces, keeping remaining dough refrigerated. With lightly floured hands, roll each piece of dough into a 7-inch-long rope; bring ends of rope together and gently twist several times. Pinch twisted ends together to seal.
3. Place cookies, 2 inches apart, on ungreased large cookie sheet. Bake cookies 12 minutes, or until bottoms are lightly browned. Transfer cookies to wire rack to cool. Repeat with remaining dough.

4. *When cookies are cool, prepare glaze:* In small bowl, mix confectioners' sugar with remaining 1 teaspoon anise extract and water. Brush cookies with glaze; place on rack. Top with sprinkles, if you like. Allow glaze to dry, about 1 hour.

# *Good Housekeeping* Gingerbread Cutouts

**Prep:** 45 minutes plus cooling and decorating
**Bake:** 12 minutes per batch    ◆    **Makes** about 3 dozen cookies

½ cup sugar
½ cup light molasses
1½ teaspoons ground ginger
1 teaspoon ground allspice
1 teaspoon ground cinnamon
1 teaspoon ground cloves
2 teaspoons baking soda
½ cup butter or margarine
    (1 stick), cut into pieces
1 large egg, beaten
3½ cups all-purpose flour
Ornamental Frosting
    (see page 96)

1. In 3-quart saucepan, combine sugar, molasses, ginger, allspice, cinnamon, and cloves and heat to boiling over medium heat, stirring occasionally. Remove saucepan from heat; stir in baking soda (mixture will foam up in the pan). Add butter and stir until melted. With fork, stir in egg, then flour. On floured surface, knead dough until well combined. Divide dough in half; wrap half in plastic wrap and set aside.
2. Preheat oven to 325°F. With floured rolling pin, roll out remaining half of dough slightly thinner than ¼ inch. With floured 3- to 4-inch assorted cookie cutters, cut dough into cookies; reserve trimmings. Place cookies, 1 inch apart, on ungreased cookie sheet. Reroll trimmings and cut out more cookies.
3. Bake 12 minutes, or until edges begin to brown. Transfer to wire racks. Repeat with remaining dough.
4. When cookies are cool, prepare Ornamental Frosting; use to decorate cookies as desired. Set cookies aside to allow frosting to dry completely, about 1 hour. If not serving right away, store cookies in airtight container.

**Each cookie without frosting:** About 90 calories, 1 g protein, 15 g carbohydrate, 3 g total fat (1 g saturated), 6 mg cholesterol, 105 mg sodium.

*PENNSYLVANIA-* ▶
*DUTCH BROWNIES,*
*MISS ELSIE'S*
*ALMOND SLICES,*
*HONEY COOKIES,*
*CHRISTMAS ROCKS,*
*AND MOM'S*
*PFEFFERNUSSE*
*(clockwise from*
*top left)*

◆

# Pennsylvania-Dutch Brownies

**Prep:** 20 minutes plus cooling   ◆   **Bake:** 15 to 20 minutes
**Makes** 30 brownies

4 tablespoons butter or margarine

1 square (1 ounce) unsweetened chocolate

¼ cup light molasses

2 large eggs

1½ cups all-purpose flour

1 teaspoon ground ginger

½ teaspoon ground cloves

½ teaspoon baking soda

½ teaspoon salt

1 cup plus 2 teaspoons sugar

1⅛ teaspoons ground cinnamon

**Each brownie:** About 80 calories, 1 g protein, 14 g carbohydrate, 2 g total fat (1 g saturated), 14 mg cholesterol, 80 mg sodium.

1. Preheat oven to 375°F. Grease 13" by 9" metal baking pan; set aside.

2. In 4-quart saucepan, melt butter with chocolate over low heat. Remove saucepan from heat. With wire whisk or fork, stir in molasses, then eggs.

3. With spoon, stir in flour, ginger, cloves, baking soda, salt, 1 cup sugar, and 1 teaspoon cinnamon just until blended. Spread batter evenly in pan. Bake 15 to 20 minutes, until toothpick inserted 2 inches from edge comes out clean.

4. Meanwhile, in cup, combine remaining 2 teaspoons sugar and ⅛ teaspoon cinnamon; set aside.

5. Remove pan from oven; immediately sprinkle brownies with cinnamon-sugar mixture. Cool brownies in pan on wire rack at least 2 hours. When cool, cut brownies lengthwise into 3 strips, then cut each strip crosswise into 5 pieces. Cut each piece diagonally in half.

# Miss Elsie's Almond Slices

**Prep:** 45 minutes plus freezing and cooling ◆ **Bake:** 15 minutes per batch
**Makes** about 24 dozen cookies

1. In large bowl, with spoon, combine melted butter and sugars. Add eggs, vanilla, lemon extract, and ground almonds; beat until well combined. Add flour, cinnamon, baking soda, salt, and nutmeg and stir until dough forms. Cover bowl with plastic wrap and freeze dough 1 hour, or until easy to handle.

2. Divide dough into 8 pieces. On lightly floured surface, with floured hands, shape each piece into a 6-inch-long log. Wrap each log in plastic wrap and freeze at least 4 hours or overnight, until firm enough to slice.

3. Preheat oven to 350°F. Grease large cookie sheet. Cut logs into very thin (about 3/16-inch) slices. Place slices, 1½ inches apart, on cookie sheet. Bake 15 minutes, or until cookies are browned. With wide spatula, transfer cookies to wire rack to cool.

1½ cups butter (3 sticks), melted
   (do not use margarine)
1 cup packed light brown sugar
1 cup granulated sugar
3 large eggs
1 teaspoon vanilla extract
½ teaspoon lemon extract
1 cup slivered almonds,
   finely ground
5½ cups all-purpose flour
2 teaspoons ground cinnamon
1½ teaspoons baking soda
1 teaspoon salt
1 teaspoon ground nutmeg

**Each cookie:** About 25 calories,
0 g protein, 3 g carbohydrate,
1 g total fat (0 g saturated),
5 mg cholesterol, 25 mg sodium.

# Mom's Pfeffernusse

**Prep:** 1 hour 30 minutes plus chilling and cooling
**Bake:** 8 to 10 minutes per batch ◆ **Makes** 20 dozen cookies

1. In large bowl, with mixer at low speed, beat sugar and eggs until blended. Increase speed to high; beat until creamy. Reduce speed to low; add flour, grated orange peel, cinnamon, allspice, baking powder, lemon extract, and cloves and beat, occasionally scraping bowl with rubber spatula, until well combined. With lightly floured hands, shape dough into 4 balls; flatten each slightly. Wrap each in plastic wrap and freeze 1 hour or refrigerate overnight. (Dough will be very sticky even after chilling.)

2. Preheat oven to 400°F. Grease large cookie sheet. On well-floured surface, with floured rolling pin, roll out 1 piece of dough into 10" by 6" rectangle, keeping remaining dough in refrigerator. With floured pastry wheel or sharp knife, cut dough lengthwise into 6 strips, then cut each strip crosswise into 10 pieces. Place cookies, about ½ inch apart, on cookie sheet.

3. Bake cookies 8 to 10 minutes, until lightly browned. With wide spatula, transfer cookies to wire racks to cool. Repeat with remaining dough.

2 cups sugar
4 large eggs
3½ cups all-purpose flour
2 tablespoons grated orange peel
1 teaspoon ground cinnamon
1 teaspoon ground allspice
1 teaspoon baking powder
1 teaspoon lemon extract
½ teaspoon ground cloves

**Each cookie:** About 15 calories,
0 g protein, 3 g carbohydrate,
0 g total fat, 4 mg cholesterol,
5 mg sodium.

# Honey Cookies

**Prep:** 40 minutes plus chilling and cooling
**Bake:** 18 to 22 minutes per batch  ◆  **Makes** about 3½ dozen cookies

1 cup butter or margarine
  (2 sticks), softened
¼ cup honey
2 teaspoons vanilla extract
2 cups all-purpose flour
2 cups walnuts, chopped
½ teaspoon salt

**Each cookie:** About 105 calories,
1 g protein, 7 g carbohydrate,
8 g total fat (1 g saturated),
0 mg cholesterol, 85 mg sodium.

1. In large bowl, with mixer at high speed, beat butter until creamy. Add honey and vanilla; beat until well blended.
2. With mixer at low speed, beat in flour, walnuts, and salt until dough forms. Cover bowl with plastic wrap and refrigerate dough at least 1 hour.
3. Preheat oven to 325°F. With lightly floured hands, shape dough by heaping teaspoons into balls. Place balls, about 2 inches apart, on ungreased large cookie sheet. Press floured 4-tine fork across top of each ball to make decorative indentations.
4. Bake cookies 18 to 22 minutes, until golden. Transfer to wire rack to cool. Repeat with remaining dough.

# Christmas Rocks

**Prep:** 45 minutes plus cooling  ◆  **Bake:** 12 to 15 minutes per batch
**Makes** about 4 dozen cookies

½ cup packed brown sugar
⅓ cup shortening
6 tablespoons butter or
  margarine, softened
2 large eggs
1½ cups all-purpose flour
1 teaspoon baking powder
1 teaspoon ground cinnamon
½ teaspoon baking soda
½ teaspoon salt
¼ teaspoon ground cloves
2 cups walnuts, coarsely chopped
2 cups dark seedless raisins
½ cup dried currants
½ cup red and/or green candied
  cherries, each cut in half
½ cup finely chopped candied
  pineapple

**Each cookie:** About 120 calories,
2 g protein, 16 g carbohydrate,
6 g total fat (1 g saturated),
9 mg cholesterol, 70 mg sodium.

1. In large bowl, with mixer at low speed, beat brown sugar, shortening, and butter, occasionally scraping bowl with rubber spatula, until mixed. Increase speed to high; beat mixture until creamy, about 2 minutes.
2. With mixer at low speed, beat in eggs, then flour, baking powder, cinnamon, baking soda, salt, and cloves just until mixed. With spoon, stir in walnuts and remaining ingredients.
3. Preheat oven to 350°F. Drop dough by rounded tablespoons, about 1½ inches apart, on ungreased large cookie sheet. Bake 12 to 15 minutes, until set and lightly browned. With wide spatula, transfer cookies to wire rack to cool. Repeat with remaining dough.

*Tip:* A one-time investment in nonstick cookie sheets will pay off in easy cleaning and fast, even baking. Pick the largest sheets that will fit in your oven, allowing 2 inches of clearance on all sides for good air circulation.

# Sally Ann Cookies

**Prep:** 1 hour plus freezing and cooling
**Bake:** 15 to 20 minutes per batch ◆ **Makes** about 12 dozen cookies

1. In large bowl, with mixer at low speed, beat sugar with butter until blended. Increase speed to high; beat until creamy. At low speed, beat in flour and remaining ingredients, except frosting and décors, until well blended. Cover bowl with plastic wrap and freeze 1 hour, or until firm enough to handle.

2. Divide dough into thirds. On lightly floured surface, shape each third into a 12-inch-long log. Wrap each log in plastic wrap and freeze at least 4 hours or overnight, until firm enough to slice.

3. Preheat oven to 350°F. Grease large cookie sheet. Cut 1 log into ¼-inch-thick slices. Place slices, about 1½ inches apart, on cookie sheet. Bake 15 to 20 minutes, until set and lightly browned around edges. Cool on cookie sheet 1 minute. With wide spatula, transfer cookies to wire rack to cool completely. Repeat with remaining dough.

4. *When cookies are cool, prepare Sally Ann Frosting:* In 2-quart saucepan, combine granulated sugar and gelatin and stir until well mixed. Stir in water; heat to boiling over high heat. Reduce heat; simmer, uncovered, 10 minutes.

5. Into small bowl, pour confectioners' sugar. With mixer at low speed, gradually add gelatin mixture to sugar and beat until well blended. Increase speed to high; beat until smooth and fluffy, with an easy spreading consistency, about 10 minutes. Beat in vanilla extract. Keep bowl covered with plastic wrap to prevent frosting from drying out.

6. With small metal spatula or knife, spread frosting on cookies. If you like, sprinkle cookies with décors. Set cookies aside to allow frosting to dry completely, about 1 hour.

*Tip:* If you would like to use *Good Housekeeping* Gingerbread Cutouts or Noël Sugar Cookies as ornaments, make 1 or 2 holes in the top of each cookie with a toothpick or straw before baking. If the holes fill in during baking, remake the holes while the cookies are still warm. After decorating, loop nylon fishing line or ribbon through for hanging.

1½ cups granulated sugar
1 cup butter or margarine
   (2 sticks)
5½ cups all-purpose flour
1 cup light molasses
½ cup cold strong coffee
2 teaspoons baking soda
2 teaspoons ground ginger
½ teaspoon ground nutmeg
½ teaspoon salt
¼ teaspoon ground cloves
holiday décors (optional)

Sally Ann Frosting
1 cup granulated sugar
1 envelope unflavored gelatin
1 cup cold water
2 cups confectioners' sugar
¼ teaspoon vanilla extract

**Each cookie without décors:**
About 55 calories, 0 g protein,
10 g carbohydrate, 1 g total fat
(0 g saturated), 0 mg cholesterol,
40 mg sodium.

# Colorful Holiday Cookies

1 cup butter or margarine
(2 sticks), slightly softened

½ cup packed light brown sugar

½ cup granulated sugar

2 large eggs

3 cups all-purpose flour

½ teaspoon baking soda

½ cup walnuts, coarsely chopped

½ cup pecans, coarsely chopped

½ cup Brazil nuts or almonds,
coarsely chopped

½ cup coarsely chopped pitted
dates

¼ cup red candied cherries

¼ cup coarsely chopped
candied pineapple

**Each cookie:** About 80 calories,
1 g protein, 9 g carbohydrate,
4 g total fat (1 g saturated),
5 mg cholesterol, 45 mg sodium.

**Prep:** 45 minutes plus chilling and cooling
**Bake:** 15 to 17 minutes per batch ◆ **Makes** about 6 dozen cookies

1. In large bowl, with mixer at low speed, beat butter with sugars, occasionally scraping bowl with rubber spatula, until blended. Increase speed to high; beat until light and fluffy, about 3 minutes. At low speed, beat in eggs until blended. Gradually beat in flour and baking soda just until mixed. With spoon, stir in walnuts and remaining ingredients.

2. Divide dough into 3 equal pieces. With floured hands, shape each piece into an 8-inch-long log. Wrap each log in plastic wrap and freeze at least 4 hours or overnight, until firm enough to slice.

3. Preheat oven to 350°F. With serrated knife, cut 1 log crosswise into about 24 slices. Place slices, about 2 inches apart, on ungreased large cookie sheet. Bake 15 to 17 minutes, until cookies are golden. With wide spatula, transfer cookies to wire rack to cool. Repeat with remaining logs.

▲ *C*OLORFUL HOLIDAY COOKIES, PEANUTTY YUMMY BARS,
AND SALLY ANN COOKIES (*clockwise from left*)

◆

# Peanutty Yummy Bars

**Prep:** 30 minutes ♦ **Bake:** 55 minutes
**Makes** 4 dozen bars

1. Preheat oven to 350°F. Grease 13" by 9" metal baking pan.
2. *Prepare crust:* In large bowl, with mixer at low speed, beat oats, 1 cup flour, ⅓ cup brown sugar, 4 tablespoons butter, and 3 tablespoons peanut butter until blended. Pat dough evenly into pan and bake 15 minutes.
3. Meanwhile, in large bowl, with mixer at medium speed, beat eggs, molasses, remaining 1½ cups brown sugar, ⅓ cup peanut butter, and 4 tablespoons butter, constantly scraping bowl with rubber spatula, until well combined. Reduce speed to low; add baking powder, salt, and remaining ⅔ cup flour and beat, occasionally scraping bowl, until blended. With spoon, stir in peanuts and chocolate pieces.
4. Spread mixture evenly over hot crust. Bake 40 minutes longer, or until golden. Cool in pan on wire rack. Dust with confectioners' sugar, if you like. When cool, cut lengthwise into 4 strips, then cut each strip crosswise into 12 pieces.

⅓ cup quick-cooking oats, uncooked
1⅔ cups all-purpose flour
⅓ cup plus 1½ cups packed light brown sugar
½ cup butter or margarine (1 stick), softened
3 tablespoons plus ⅓ cup chunky peanut butter
3 large eggs
4½ teaspoons light molasses
2 teaspoons baking powder
½ teaspoon salt
1 cup salted cocktail peanuts, chopped
1 package (6 ounces) semisweet chocolate pieces (1 cup)
confectioners' sugar for garnish (optional)

**Each bar:** About 125 calories, 3 g protein, 16 g carbohydrate, 6 g total fat (1 g saturated), 13 mg cholesterol, 100 mg sodium.

# Finska Kakor

**Prep:** 1 hour plus cooling ♦ **Bake:** 17 to 20 minutes per batch
**Makes** 64 bars

1. In food processor with knife blade attached, process almonds with 2 tablespoons sugar until almonds are finely chopped; set aside.
2. Into large bowl, measure flour, butter, almond extract, and remaining ½ cup sugar. With hand, knead ingredients until well blended and mixture holds together.
3. Preheat oven to 350°F. On work surface, between 2 sheets of waxed paper, roll out half of dough into 12" by 8" rectangle. With pastry brush, brush dough rectangle with some egg white. Sprinkle with half of almond mixture. With rolling pin, gently press almonds into dough.
4. Cut dough rectangle lengthwise into 8 strips. Cut each strip crosswise into 4 bars. With wide spatula, place bars, about ½ inch apart, on ungreased large cookie sheet.
5. Bake bars 17 to 20 minutes, until lightly browned. Transfer to wire rack to cool. Repeat with remaining dough.

1 cup blanched almonds
2 tablespoons plus ½ cup sugar
4 cups all-purpose flour
1½ cups butter or margarine (3 sticks), softened
2 teaspoons almond extract
1 egg white, beaten

**Each bar:** About 85 calories, 1 g protein, 8 g carbohydrate, 5 g total fat (1 g saturated), 0 mg cholesterol, 60 mg sodium.

# Noisettines

1 package (3 ounces) cream
   cheese, softened
½ cup (1 stick) plus 1 tablespoon
   butter or margarine, softened
1 cup all-purpose flour
1⅓ cups hazelnuts (filberts)
⅔ cup packed light brown sugar
1 large egg
1 teaspoon vanilla extract

**Each cookie:** About 135 calories,
2 g protein, 11 g carbohydrate,
10 g total fat (2 g saturated),
13 mg cholesterol, 75 mg sodium.

**Prep:** 1 hour plus chilling and cooling    ◆    **Bake:** 30 minutes
**Makes** 2 dozen cookies

1. In large bowl, with mixer at high speed, beat cream cheese with ½ cup butter until creamy. Reduce speed to low; add flour and beat until well combined. Cover bowl with plastic wrap and refrigerate 30 minutes.
2. Meanwhile, preheat oven to 350°F. Place hazelnuts in 9" by 9" metal baking pan. Bake 10 to 15 minutes until toasted. Wrap hot hazelnuts in clean cloth towel. With hands, roll hazelnuts back and forth to remove skins. Cool completely.
3. Reserve 24 hazelnuts for garnish. In food processor with knife blade attached, process remaining hazelnuts with brown sugar until nuts are finely ground.
4. In medium bowl, with spoon, combine hazelnut mixture with egg, vanilla, and remaining 1 tablespoon butter.
5. With floured hands, divide chilled dough into 24 equal pieces (dough will be very soft). Gently press each piece of dough evenly onto bottom and up sides of 24 ungreased miniature muffin-pan cups. Spoon filling by heaping teaspoons into each pastry cup; place 1 whole hazelnut on top of filling in each cup.
6. Bake 30 minutes, or until filling is set and crust is golden. With tip of knife, loosen cookie cups from muffin-pan cups and place on wire rack to cool completely.

# Horns

1 cup butter or margarine
   (2 sticks)
2½ cups all-purpose flour
1 container (8 ounces) sour cream
1 large egg yolk
¾ cup sugar
¾ cup walnuts, finely chopped
1½ teaspoons ground cinnamon
confectioners' sugar for garnish

**Each cookie:** About 55 calories,
1 g protein, 5 g carbohydrate,
4 g total fat (1 g saturated),
4 mg cholesterol, 30 mg sodium.

**Prep:** 1 hour 30 minutes plus freezing and cooling
**Bake:** 20 minutes per batch    ◆    **Makes** 80 cookies

1. In large bowl, with pastry blender or 2 knives used scissor-fashion, cut butter into flour until fine crumbs form. In cup, with fork, mix sour cream and egg yolk. Stir sour-cream mixture into flour mixture just until blended and dough comes away from side of bowl (dough will be sticky). Cover bowl with plastic wrap and freeze 1 hour, or until firm enough to handle.
2. Divide dough into 5 equal pieces. On lightly floured surface, shape each piece into a disk. Wrap each disk in plastic wrap and freeze at least 4 hours or overnight, until firm enough to roll.

3. In small bowl, combine sugar, walnuts, and cinnamon. On sheet of lightly floured waxed paper, with floured rolling pin, roll out 1 piece of dough into a 12-inch round, keeping remaining dough refrigerated. Sprinkle dough with rounded ¼ cup walnut mixture; gently press into dough. With pastry wheel or sharp knife, cut dough into 16 equal wedges. Starting at curved edge, roll up each wedge, jelly-roll fashion. Place cookies, point side down, 1½ inches apart, on ungreased cookie sheet. Shape each into a crescent. Repeat with remaining dough, one-fifth at a time.

4. Preheat oven to 350°F. Bake cookies 20 minutes, or until golden. With wide spatula, transfer cookies to wire rack to cool. When cookies are cool, sprinkle with confectioners' sugar.

▲ *N*OISETTINES, HORNS,
AND FINSKA KAKOR
*(clockwise from top left)*

◆

# Noël Sugar Cookies

¾ cup sugar

10 tablespoons butter
(1¼ sticks), softened

1 teaspoon baking powder

½ teaspoon salt

2 tablespoons milk

2 teaspoons vanilla extract

1 large egg

2 cups all-purpose flour

Ornamental Frosting
(see page 96)

**Each cookie without frosting:**
About 55 calories, 1 g protein,
7 g carbohydrate, 3 g total fat
(2 g saturated), 11 mg cholesterol,
55 mg sodium.

**Prep:** 45 minutes plus chilling, cooling, and decorating

**Bake:** 12 to 15 minutes per batch    ◆    **Makes** about 4 dozen cookies

1. In large bowl, with mixer at low speed, beat sugar, butter, baking powder, and salt until blended. Increase speed to high; beat until light and fluffy. Reduce speed to low; add milk, vanilla, and egg and beat until blended. (Mixture may appear curdled.)

2. With wooden spoon, stir in flour until blended. Shape dough into 2 balls; flatten each slightly. Wrap each with plastic wrap and refrigerate 1 hour, or until dough is easy to handle. (Or, place dough in freezer 30 minutes.)

3. Preheat oven to 350°F. On lightly floured surface, with floured rolling pin, roll out 1 piece of dough ⅛ inch thick, keeping remaining dough refrigerated. With floured 3- to 4-inch assorted cookie cutters, cut dough into as many cookies as possible; reserve trimmings. Place cookies, about 1 inch apart, on 2 ungreased large cookie sheets. Reroll trimmings and cut out more cookies.

4. Bake cookies on 2 oven racks 12 to 15 minutes, until golden around edges, rotating cookie sheets between upper and lower racks halfway through baking time. With wide spatula, transfer cookies to wire racks to cool. Repeat with remaining dough.

5. When cookies are cool, prepare Ornamental Frosting; use to decorate cookies as desired. Set cookies aside to allow frosting to dry completely, at least 1 hour. If not using right away, store in tightly covered container.

# Vinegar Cookies

1 cup butter or margarine
(2 sticks), softened

1 cup sugar

1½ cups all-purpose flour

1 tablespoon distilled
white vinegar

½ teaspoon baking soda

**Each cookie:** About 65 calories,
0 g protein, 7 g carbohydrate,
4 g total fat (1 g saturated),
0 mg cholesterol, 50 mg sodium.

**Prep:** 25 minutes plus chilling and cooling

**Bake:** 17 to 20 minutes per batch    ◆    **Makes** about 4 dozen cookies

1. In large bowl, with mixer at low speed, beat butter with sugar until blended. Increase speed to high; beat until light and fluffy, about 3 minutes. At low speed, beat in flour, vinegar, and baking soda, occasionally scraping bowl with rubber spatula, until mixed. Cover bowl with plastic wrap and refrigerate dough 1 hour, or until easy to handle.

2. Preheat oven to 350°F. Drop dough by rounded teaspoons, about 2 inches apart, onto ungreased large cookie sheet. Bake 17 to 20 minutes,

until cookies are set and edges are golden. Let cookies remain on cookie sheet 30 seconds, then with wide spatula, transfer cookies to wire rack to cool completely. Repeat with remaining dough.

# Greek Cinnamon Paximadia

**Prep:** 1 hour plus cooling  ◆  **Bake:** 50 minutes
**Makes** about 4 dozen cookies

1. In large bowl, with mixer at low speed, beat butter, shortening, and 1 cup sugar until blended. Increase speed to high; beat until light and fluffy, about 5 minutes. At low speed, add eggs, 1 at a time, then vanilla, and beat until well mixed.

2. Gradually add baking powder, baking soda, and 3 cups flour and beat until well blended. With wooden spoon, stir in remaining 1 cup flour until soft dough forms. If necessary, add additional flour (up to ½ cup) until dough is easy to handle.

3. Preheat oven to 350°F. Divide dough into 4 equal pieces. On lightly floured surface, shape each piece of dough into an 8-inch-long log. Place 2 logs, about 4 inches apart, on each of 2 ungreased large cookie sheets. Flatten each log to 2½ inches wide.

4. Place cookie sheets on 2 oven racks and bake logs 20 minutes, or until lightly browned and toothpick inserted in center comes out clean, rotating cookie sheets between upper and lower racks halfway through baking time. Meanwhile, in pie plate, mix cinnamon with remaining ½ cup sugar.

5. Remove cookie sheets from oven. Transfer hot loaves (during baking, logs will spread and become loaves) to cutting board; with serrated knife, cut diagonally into ½-inch-thick slices. Coat slices with cinnamon-sugar. Return slices, cut side down, to same cookie sheets. Bake slices 15 minutes. Turn slices over and return to oven, rotating cookie sheets between upper and lower racks, and bake 15 minutes longer, or until golden. With wide spatula, transfer cookies to wire racks to cool.

½ cup butter or margarine
   (1 stick), softened
½ cup shortening
1½ cups sugar
3 large eggs
1 tablespoon vanilla extract
2 teaspoons baking powder
½ teaspoon baking soda
about 4 cups all-purpose flour
1½ teaspoons ground cinnamon

**Each cookie:** About 105 calories, 1 g protein, 14 g carbohydrate, 5 g total fat (1 g saturated), 13 mg cholesterol, 60 mg sodium.

# Chocolate Sambuca Cookies

12 squares (1 ounce each)
   semisweet chocolate

4 tablespoons butter or margarine

3 large eggs

⅓ cup sambuca (anise-flavored
   liqueur)

1 cup granulated sugar

1 cup blanched almonds,
   finely ground

⅔ cup all-purpose flour

¾ teaspoon baking soda

⅓ cup confectioners' sugar

**Each cookie:** About 85 calories,
2 g protein, 12 g carbohydrate,
4 g total fat (0 g saturated),
13 mg cholesterol, 20 mg sodium.

**Prep:** 30 minutes plus chilling and cooling
**Bake:** 10 to 12 minutes per batch    ◆    **Makes** about 4 dozen cookies

1. In 2-quart saucepan, melt chocolate with butter over low heat, stirring frequently. Remove saucepan from heat; cool chocolate mixture slightly.

2. In medium bowl, with wire whisk, mix eggs, sambuca, and ½ cup granulated sugar; blend in chocolate mixture. With spoon, stir ground almonds, flour, and baking soda into chocolate mixture until combined (dough will be very soft). Cover bowl with plastic wrap and refrigerate at least 4 hours or overnight.

3. Preheat oven to 350°F. In small bowl, combine confectioners' sugar and remaining ½ cup granulated sugar. With lightly floured hands, roll dough by rounded tablespoons into balls. Roll balls in sugar mixture to coat. Place balls, about 2 inches apart, on ungreased large cookie sheet. Bake 10

𝒢REEK ▶
CINNAMON
PAXIMADIA,
VINEGAR COOKIES,
AND
CHOCOLATE
SAMBUCA COOKIES
*(from top right)*

◆

to 12 minutes, until cookies are just set and look puffed and cracked. Let cookies remain on cookie sheet 1 minute to cool slightly. With wide spatula, transfer to wire rack to cool completely. Repeat with remaining dough and sugar mixture.

# Czechoslovakian Cookies

**Prep:** 25 minutes plus cooling  ◆  **Bake:** 45 to 50 minutes
**Makes** 30 bars

1. Preheat oven to 350°F. Grease 9" by 9" metal baking pan.
2. In large bowl, with mixer at low speed, beat butter and sugar, occasionally scraping bowl with rubber spatula, until mixed. Increase speed to high; beat until light and fluffy.
3. With mixer at low speed, beat in egg yolks, constantly scraping bowl with rubber spatula, until well combined. Add flour and salt and beat, occasionally scraping bowl, until blended. Stir in walnuts.
4. With lightly floured hands, pat half of dough evenly into bottom of pan. Spread strawberry preserves over dough. With lightly floured hands, pinch off ¾-inch pieces from remaining dough and drop over preserves; do not pat down.
5. Bake 45 to 50 minutes, until golden. Cool completely in pan on wire rack. When cool, cut into 3 strips, then cut each strip crosswise into 10 pieces.

1 cup butter (2 sticks), softened
  (do not use margarine)
1 cup sugar
2 large egg yolks
2 cups all-purpose flour
pinch salt
1 cup walnuts, chopped
½ cup strawberry preserves

**Each bar:** About 130 calories,
2 g protein, 11 g carbohydrate,
9 g total fat (4 g saturated),
31 mg cholesterol, 70 mg sodium.

# Hazelnut Cookies

**Prep:** 1 hour plus cooling  ◆  **Bake:** 25 minutes per batch
**Makes** about 4 dozen sandwich cookies

1. Preheat oven to 350°F. Place nuts in 13" by 9" metal baking pan. Bake 10 to 15 minutes, until toasted. Wrap hot hazelnuts in clean cloth towel. With hands, roll hazelnuts back and forth to remove skins. Cool completely.
2. Turn oven control to 275°F. Grease 2 large cookie sheets. In food processor with knife blade attached, process hazelnuts with ¼ cup sugar until nuts are finely ground.

2 cups hazelnuts (filberts)
¾ cup sugar
5 large egg whites
⅓ cup all-purpose flour
5 tablespoons butter or
  margarine, melted and cooled
6 squares (6 ounces) semisweet
  chocolate, melted and cooled

**Each sandwich cookie:**
About 75 calories, 1 g protein,
7 g carbohydrate, 5 g total fat
(0 g saturated), 0 mg cholesterol,
25 mg sodium.

3. In large bowl, with mixer at high speed, beat egg whites until soft peaks form. Beating at high speed, sprinkle in remaining ½ cup sugar, 1 tablespoon at a time, beating well after each addition until sugar completely dissolves and whites stand in stiff peaks. With rubber spatula, fold in ground hazelnuts, flour, and melted butter or margarine.

4. Drop mixture by rounded teaspoons, about 2 inches apart, onto cookie sheets. Bake cookies on 2 oven racks 25 minutes, rotating cookie sheets between upper and lower racks halfway through baking time, or until cookies are firm and edges are golden. With wide spatula, transfer to wire racks to cool. Repeat with remaining batter.

5. When cookies are cool, with small metal spatula, spread thin layer of melted chocolate onto flat side of half of cookies. Top with remaining cookies, flat side down, to make sandwiches. Spoon remaining chocolate into small zip-tight plastic bag; snip 1 corner of bag to make small hole. Squeeze thin lines of chocolate over cookies. Let stand until set.

▲ *C*ZECHOSLOVAKIAN COOKIES, HAZELNUT COOKIES, AND WOODEN-SPOON COOKIES
*(clockwise from right on plate)*

◆

¾ cup blanched almonds, ground
½ cup butter or margarine (1 stick), softened
½ cup sugar
1 tablespoon all-purpose flour
1 tablespoon heavy or whipping cream

**Each cookie:** About 50 calories, 1 g protein, 3 g carbohydrate, 4 g total fat (1 g saturated), 1 mg cholesterol, 35 mg sodium.

# Wooden-Spoon Cookies

**Prep:** 25 minutes plus cooling     ◆     **Bake:** 5 to 7 minutes per batch
**Makes** about 3 dozen cookies

1. Preheat oven to 350°F. Grease and flour 2 large cookie sheets. In 2-quart saucepan, combine ground almonds, butter, sugar, flour, and cream. Heat over low heat, stirring occasionally, until butter melts. Keep mixture warm over very low heat.

2. Drop batter by rounded teaspoons, about 3 inches apart, onto cookie sheet. (Do not place more than 6 cookies on sheet because, after baking, cookies must be shaped quickly before they harden.)

3. Bake cookies 5 to 7 minutes, until edges are lightly browned and centers are golden. Let cookies remain on cookie sheet 30 to 60 seconds, until edges are set. With long, flexible metal spatula, flip cookies over quickly so lacy texture will be on outside after rolling. Working as quickly as possible, roll each cookie into a cylinder around handle of wooden spoon; transfer to wire rack. If cookies become too hard to roll, return to oven briefly to soften. As each cookie is shaped, remove from spoon handle; cool on wire rack. Repeat until all batter is used.

# Ricotta-Cheese Cookies

**Prep:** 30 minutes plus cooling ◆ **Bake:** 15 minutes per batch
**Makes** about 6 dozen cookies

1. Preheat oven to 350°F. In large bowl, with mixer at low speed, beat granulated sugar with butter until blended. Increase speed to high; beat until light and fluffy, about 5 minutes. At medium speed, beat in ricotta, vanilla, and eggs until well combined. Reduce speed to low. Add flour, baking powder, and salt; beat until dough forms.

2. Drop dough by level tablespoons, about 2 inches apart, onto ungreased large cookie sheet. Bake about 15 minutes, until cookies are very lightly golden (cookies will be soft). Transfer cookies to wire rack to cool. Repeat with remaining dough.

3. ***When cookies are cool, prepare icing:*** In small bowl, stir confectioners' sugar and milk until smooth. With small metal spatula or knife, spread icing on cookies; sprinkle with red or green sugar crystals. Set cookies aside to allow icing to dry completely, about 1 hour.

*Tip:* Here are a few simple strategies to make your holiday cookie-baking fast, efficient, and fun!

- Pick user-friendly equipment like nonstick cookie sheets and smooth-gliding rolling pins with ball bearings in the handles.

- Whip up a batch of dough and divide it into small portions (for faster defrosting). Wrap each portion in foil and place in a labeled, heavy-weight plastic bag. Freeze for up to 2 months. Slice-and-bake cookie dough can be used without defrosting; other doughs require a couple of hours in the refrigerator or on the kitchen counter.

- For even faster baking, freeze uncooked drop cookies on their pan, then transfer them to freezer bags. Take out enough to fill a sheet (for a small batch use your toaster oven), let warm to room temperature, then bake.

- Start your holiday baking early! Baked, iced, and decorated cookies store well frozen for up to 3 months. To freeze baked cookies, bake them completely, cool, and pack them between layers of waxed paper in airtight freezer containers. To prevent sogginess, don't forget to unwrap them before thawing.

- Save cleanup time by lining cookie sheets with foil; it can be greased just as you would the pan. For bar cookies, extend a sheet of foil over the edges of the pan. After cooling, remove the whole batch at once, lifting the foil by its edges and placing it on a cutting board.

- Set up a production line: While one batch bakes, cut a sheet of foil and place unbaked cookies on it. When the first batch is done, slide the foil onto a rack, cool the baking sheet slightly, and slide the second sheet of foil on to bake.

2 cups granulated sugar
1 cup butter or margarine
   (2 sticks), softened
1 container (15 ounces) ricotta
   cheese
2 teaspoons vanilla extract
2 large eggs
4 cups all-purpose flour
2 tablespoons baking powder
1 teaspoon salt
1½ cups confectioners' sugar
3 tablespoons milk
red and green sugar crystals

**Each cookie:** About 90 calories,
1 g protein, 14 g carbohydrate,
3 g total fat (1 g saturated),
3 mg cholesterol, 100 mg sodium.

# Cinnamon Twists

1 package (8 ounces) cream
  cheese, softened
1 cup butter or margarine
  (2 sticks), softened
2½ cups all-purpose flour
¾ cup walnuts
1 cup sugar
2 teaspoons ground cinnamon
1 large egg, beaten

**Each cookie:** About 75 calories,
1 g protein, 7 g carbohydrate,
5 g total fat (1 g saturated),
7 mg cholesterol, 50 mg sodium.

**Prep:** 1 hour plus chilling and cooling
**Bake:** 15 to 17 minutes per batch   ◆   **Makes** 5½ dozen cookies

1. In large bowl, with mixer at low speed, beat cream cheese with butter, constantly scraping bowl with rubber spatula, until blended. Increase speed to high; beat until light and creamy, about 2 minutes. With mixer at low speed, gradually add 1 cup flour and beat until blended. With spoon, stir in remaining 1½ cups flour until smooth.

2. On lightly floured sheet of plastic wrap, pat dough into a 9" by 9" square. Wrap in plastic wrap and refrigerate 2 hours, or until firm enough to roll.

3. Meanwhile, in food processor with knife blade attached, process walnuts with ¼ cup sugar until walnuts are finely ground. In small bowl, combine cinnamon and remaining ¾ cup sugar with walnut mixture and stir until well blended; set aside.

4. Preheat oven to 400°F. Grease large cookie sheet. On lightly floured sheet of waxed paper, with floured rolling pin, roll out dough square into 11" by 10½" rectangle. With pastry brush, brush some beaten egg over top of dough rectangle; sprinkle with half of walnut mixture. Gently press walnut mixture into dough. Invert dough rectangle, nut side down, onto another sheet of lightly floured waxed paper. Brush with beaten egg; sprinkle with remaining walnut mixture and gently press nut mixture into dough.

5. Cut dough lengthwise into three 3½-inch-wide bars, then crosswise into ½-inch-wide strips to make sixty-six 3½" by ½" strips. Twist each strip twice, then place, 1 inch apart, on cookie sheet.

6. Bake twists 15 to 17 minutes, until lightly browned. With wide spatula, loosen twists from cookie sheet and transfer to wire rack to cool. Repeat with remaining strips.

# Greek Christmas Cookies

**Prep:** 50 minutes plus cooling  ◆  **Bake:** 15 minutes per batch
**Makes** about 6 dozen cookies

1. Preheat oven to 350°F. In large bowl, with mixer at low speed, beat butter with confectioners' sugar until blended. Increase speed to high; beat until light and creamy. At low speed, beat in flour, cinnamon, nutmeg, cloves, salt, and egg yolk. Knead in almonds.

2. Roll dough into 1-inch balls (dough will be crumbly). Place balls, 2 inches apart, on ungreased large cookie sheet. Gently press a cherry half on top of each ball. Bake 15 minutes, or until bottoms of cookies are lightly browned. With wide spatula, transfer cookies to wire rack to cool. Repeat with remaining dough and cherries.

1 cup butter or margarine
   (2 sticks)
2 cups confectioners' sugar
2 cups all-purpose flour
1 teaspoon ground cinnamon
½ teaspoon ground nutmeg
½ teaspoon ground cloves
⅛ teaspoon salt
1 large egg yolk
2 cups blanched almonds, ground
about 1 cup red candied cherries,
   each cut in half

**Each cookie:** About 75 calories,
1 g protein, 9 g carbohydrate,
4 g total fat (1 g saturated),
3 mg cholesterol, 40 mg sodium.

◀ *C*INNAMON TWISTS,
RICOTTA-CHEESE
COOKIES, AND GREEK
CHRISTMAS COOKIES
*(clockwise from left
on plate)*

◆

# Children's Party

## Little Cookie Houses

Assorted large crackers and cookies (such as Wasa Crisps and Social Teas) for building, plus sugar wafers and round, scalloped butter cookies for decorating

1 batch Ornamental Frosting (see page 96) or 1 tub (16 ounces) ready-to-use decorator icing

Assorted decorations and colorful candies, including pretzel sticks, ice cream cones, Necco wafers, Starlight mints, M&M's, gumdrops, Mike & Ike candy, mini Chiclets, and red hots

1. Assemble houses or other structures from large crackers or cookies, attaching pieces with Ornamental Frosting. (Frosting recipe makes 3 cups; you may need more or less, depending on how houses are decorated.) Spread frosting on cookie edges; hold edges together for a few minutes until set. (If the party is for small children, you may want to assemble some houses before they arrive.)

2. Decorate as desired. For log cabin, ice outer walls and attach pretzel sticks. For church, make steeple from iced sugar wafer, with pretzel cross at top; make doors from sugar wafers trimmed at top with knife. Decorate roofs with assorted candies. For Necco-wafer shingles, spread roof generously with frosting. Starting at bottom of roof, arrange wafers so they overlap slightly. Use upside-down ice cream cones for castle turrets: Spread with frosting and sprinkle with multicolored nonpareils. Attach decorations with Ornamental Frosting.

# Gingerbread Candyland Cottage

## Materials

Gingersnap Dough (see below)

2 batches Ornamental Frosting (see page 96)

Poster board, cardboard, or foam core for patterns plus paper

6 disposable decorating bags

6 couplers

#2 thin writing decorating tip (1/32-inch opening)

#3 writing decorating tip (1/16-inch opening)

#25 star decorating tip (1/2-inch opening)

#65 leaf decorating tip (smallest available)

brown, red, blue, green, and black food-color pastes

nontoxic marker

1 piece (9½" by 10½" or larger) foam core, 3/16 inch thick or 2 layers heavy cardboard glued together

1 bag (8 ounces) plain candy-coated chocolate candies

## Roll, Cut, and Bake

### Gingersnap Dough

1½ cups heavy or whipping cream

2½ cups packed brown sugar

1¼ cups molasses

1 tablespoon ground ginger

1 tablespoon grated lemon peel

2 tablespoons baking soda

9 cups all-purpose flour

*This festive fantasy of gingerbread, icing, and candy requires only 6 shaped pattern pieces.*

1. *To prepare the dough:* Whip cream. Add sugar, molasses, ginger, lemon peel, and baking soda. Stir 10 minutes. Add flour and work with hands until smooth. Cover and refrigerate overnight.

2. *To roll dough:* Roll out on greased and floured 17" by 14" cookie sheets (placing 3/16-inch or 1/8-inch dowels on either side will help you roll out dough to uniform thickness.) Before cutting shapes, chill rolled dough on cookie sheets in refrigerator or freezer. Rechill as necessary to keep it "leather hard," which makes it easier to cut.

3. *To make patterns:* Enlarge diagrams to full size and cut patterns from poster board, heavy cardboard, or foam core.

4. *To cut and bake:* Flour patterns. Using pizza wheel or sharp knife, cut out cottage pieces, leaving at least ½ inch between them. Remove scraps (they can be rerolled, though the cookies won't be as smooth). Chill cutout pieces for 10 minutes. Brush dough with water before baking. Preheat oven to 300°F and bake 25 to 30 minutes or until firm to the touch. While gingerbread is still warm, place patterns on top again and trim shapes to match if necessary. Let cool on cookie sheets.

## Decorate

1. *Windows and Door:* Trace pattern pieces on paper; cut out windows and door from paper to create a stencil. Place stencil on gingerbread. Trace outline of windows and door using a nontoxic marker.

2. *Roof:* Using nontoxic marker and following design on roof pattern, draw 6 rows of garland on each half of roof.

3. Make 1 batch of Ornamental Frosting and divide among 5 containers. Tint 1 dark brown, 1 red, 1 light blue, 1 green, and let 1 remain white. Decorate cottage using frosting, decorating bags, and specified tips. Be

sure to cover each bowl of frosting with plastic wrap until using so it does not dry out.

4. With dark-brown frosting and #2 writing tip, outline windows, shutters, door, door hinges, and white trim on front of cottage. Pipe frosting over rows of garland on roof. Let dry.

5. Reserve 1 tablespoon red frosting. Thin the remaining red frosting with less than ½ teaspoon water until it is of spreading consistency. Check by dropping a teaspoon of frosting back into the bowl. If the dropped frosting disappears by the time you count to ten, the frosting is the right consistency. If the frosting mounds and is still visible, add a few more drops of water. Using #2 tip, fill in shutters and door with thinned red frosting. Let dry.

6. With blue frosting and #3 writing tip, pipe a row of blue dots, some big, some small, below each window and around door. Thin remaining blue frosting as in step 5. Using #2 tip, fill in windows and small window on the door. Let dry.

7. With green frosting and #3 tip, pipe green dots around tops of windows. With #65 small leaf tip, pipe wreath above door. With reserved red frosting and #2 tip, pipe red dots on wreath; make vertical lines on door.

8. Thin half of white frosting as in step 5 and using #2 tip, fill in white trim on cottage front. Let dry. Using #3 tip, pipe wavy brown design on top of white trim.

9. Using green frosting and #3 tip, pipe 3 rows of green garland on each half of roof over brown frosting. Using white frosting and #2 tip, pipe rows of white dots on roof. Let dry.

10. Mix the remaining white frosting and some of the brown frosting to make tan. Using tan frosting and #2 tip, pipe dots for center of folk-art designs above and below windows and around white trim. Then pipe teardrop shapes with green, tan, and brown frosting around the tan dots. Using tan

frosting and #3 tip, pipe 3 rows of tan garland on each roof half in between rows of green garland. Attach candy-coated chocolate candies between rows of garland, using frosting. Using tan frosting and #2 tip, pipe crisscrosses on windowpanes and on door window; make doorknob.

11. Mix all remaining colors together and add a little black food-color paste. Using #2 tip, pipe vertical lines on shutters and hinges on door. Let all pieces dry overnight before assembling.

### Assemble

1. Make the second batch of Ornamental Frosting. Using #25 star tip, pipe a thick band of frosting on the bottom and side edges of the front piece. Place it upright on the foam core (position it so cottage will be centered on foam core). Ice edges of the 2 side pieces and attach to front. (Carefully place heavy cans against pieces to support structure

◆ *Roof (Cut 2)*

◆ *Front and Back (Cut 2)*

◆ *Sides (Cut 2)*

◆ *Each square equals 1 inch. Connect lines across pattern pieces to form a grid. Or enlarge patterns 400 percent using a copy machine.*

while you work.) Ice edges of cottage back and attach to sides. Let dry for a few hours.

2. Using #25 star tip, pipe frosting along top edge of cottage and top of roof pieces. Place roof pieces on cottage; hold or prop up until frosting sets. With a dab of frosting on each, attach candy-coated chocolate candies in rows along roof peak and down diagonal roof edges; pipe dots of green frosting between candy-coated chocolate candies.

3. Cover exposed foam core with white frosting to resemble snow. Make cobblestone path in front of door: Using #3 tip and remaining dark frosting, pipe unmatched dots to resemble cobblestones. Pipe a row of small uniform dots along exposed wall seams.

# Centerpieces

▲ CRANBERRY FLORAL
CENTERPIECE P. 122

## Floral and Candle Centerpiece

*The bright purple-pink and red of the anemones in this grouping are deftly highlighted by the light green of the limes and the warm brown tones of the cinnamon sticks.*

1. Submerge oasis in water until saturated. Allow to drain, then cut into 3" squares.
2. Arrange candles and cinnamon sticks on platter.
3. Place blocks of oasis between candles, and fill with flowers and greens.
4. Finish with pine cones and limes.

**Materials**
**Block of oasis**
**Pillar candles**
**Cinnamon sticks**
**Oval platter**
**Fresh flowers and greens such as anemones, ranunculus, eucalyptus, and cedar**
**Pine cones**
**Limes**

# Cranberry Floral Centerpiece

*Use cranberries instead of florists' marbles to hold stems in a crystal vase and experiment with different combinations of fresh flowers and greenery.*

**Materials**

Glass cylinder vase

Fresh or frozen
whole cranberries

Assorted fresh flowers such as
roses, hyacinth, tulips, and
paperwhites

1. Partially fill container with water; add cranberries.
2. Arrange flowers, hiding stems in berries. Depending on amount of displacement, you may need to add or remove some berries.

# Hurricane Lamp Floral Centerpiece

*A quaint hurricane lamp, rising up as if from an island paradise, anchors this arrangement to your table. The trailing ivy provides movement and visual flow.*

1. Submerge oasis ring in water until saturated. Allow to drain.
2. Cut and insert greens.
3. Cut and insert flowers.
4. Place around base of hurricane lantern.

Materials

12" oasis ring
Assorted greens, flowers and
  herbs such as eucalyptus, ivy,
  rosemary, anemones, and
  ranunculus

# Gilded Pear Place Marker

**Materials**
**Plaid Treasure Gold**
**Pear with stem**
**Small blank card**
**Gold marker**
**Hole punch**
**Ribbon**

*Beckon your guests to the table by name with beguiling golden-pear place markers.*

1. Use finger to apply Treasure Gold to pear. Allow to dry.
2. Write guest's name on card with gold marker. Punch hole in one corner.
3. Attach card to pear stem with ribbon.

## Good Housekeeping
## Metric Conversion Chart

| Volume | | Temperature | | Weight | |
|---|---|---|---|---|---|
| | | *(To convert from Fahrenheit to Celsius: subtract 32, multiply by 5, then divide by 9.)* | | | |
| 1 teaspoon | 5 ml | | | 1 ounce | 28.3 grams |
| 1 tablespoon | 15 ml | | | 4 ounces | 113 grams |
| ¼ cup | 60 ml | 32°F | 0°C | 8 ounces | 227 grams |
| ⅓ cup | 80 ml | 212°F | 100°C | 12 ounces | 340.2 grams |
| ½ cup | 120 ml | 250°F | 121°C | 1 pound | .45 kilo |
| ⅔ cup | 160 ml | 325°F | 163°C | 2 pounds, 3¼ ounces | 1 kilo (1,000 grams) |
| ¾ cup | 180 ml | 350°F | 176°C | | |
| 1 cup | 240 ml | 375°F | 190°C | | |
| 1 pint (U.S.) | 475 ml | 400°F | 205°C | | |
| 1 quart | .95 liter | 425°F | 218°C | | |
| 1 quart plus ¼ cup | 1 liter | 450°F | 232°C | | |
| 1 gallon (U.S.) | 3.8 liters | | | | |

## Acknowledgments
Octine Arcoroc Salad Plate: Courtesy of Cardinal International, Inc.

## Photography Credits
Peter Ardito: pages 86, 88, 92
Mary Ellen Bartley: page 87
Brian Hagiwara: front cover, top right and bottom right; back cover, bottom left; pages 10 (second from left), 17, 26, 30, 32, 45, 49, 56, 58, 63, 73, 79, 119
John Kane: pages 118, 126
Kevin Lein: page 125
Peter Margonelli: pages 2–3, 8
Keith Scott Morton: pages 1, 4, 6, 7, 10 (top left), 121 (bottom), 122, 123, 124, 128
David Murray and Jules Selmes: pages 13, 15
Steven Mark Needham: pages 5 (top), 11, 12, 16, 19
Alan Richardson: front cover, top left; back cover, top right; pages 5 (second and third from top), 10 (far right), 36, 50, 57, 64, 65, 69, 71, 75, 78, 81, 116, 117
Ann Stratton: pages 21, 22
Mark Thomas: front cover, bottom left; back cover, top left and bottom right; spine; pages 5 (bottom), 9, 10 (far left and third from left), 26, 28, 31, 35, 37, 39, 40, 43, 46, 94, 95, 97, 100, 104, 107, 110, 112, 115

## Photo Styling *(Commissioned photographs)*
Richard Kollath: pages 1, 4, 6, 10 (top left), 121 (bottom), 122, 123, 124

## Designers
Richard Kollath: Dried Florals in Basket, page 1; Berries in Silver Horn, page 4; Mixed Greens Wreath, page 5; Floral and Candle Centerpiece, page 121; Cranberry Floral Centerpiece, page 122; Hurricane Lamp Floral Centerpiece, page 123; Gilded Pear Place Marker, page 124.
Matthew Mead: Christmas Stockings, page 125.

## Cookie Recipe Credits
The following cookie recipes first appeared in the December 1996 issue of *Good Housekeeping* as winners of a contest announced and promoted in *Good Housekeeping*. The recipes have been adapted and tested by the *Good Housekeeping* Test Kitchen.
Page 94: Sand Tarts, Vivian A. Eck, Williamsport, PA.
Page 96: Great-Granny's Old-Time Spice Cookies, Shirley A. Fisher, Bethlehem, PA.
Page 97: Jelly Centers, Ann Marie Reinle, Massapequa, NY.
Page 98: Layered Date Bars, Mary Beth Rollick, Munroe Falls, OH.
Page 98: Aunt Tess's Anisette Cookies, Ann Cullen, Wantagh, NY.
Page 100: Pennsylvania-Dutch Brownies, Yvonne D. Kanoff, Mount Joy, PA;
Page 101: Miss Elsie's Almond Slices, Ann Wood, Columbia, MD.
Page 101: Mom's Pfeffernusse, Carol A. Buck, Sherman Oaks, CA.
Page 102: Honey Cookies, Dawn Zimmerman, Couderay, WI.

Page 102: Christmas Rocks, Betty Pfeifer, Bay Village, OH.
Page 103: Sally Ann Cookies, Sue Riesterer, Manitowoc, WI.
Page 104: Colorful Holiday Cookies, Loretta Rakofsky, Dallas, TX.
Page 105: Peanutty Yummy Bars, Susanne Corker, Lake Orion, MI.
Page 105: Finska Kakor, Sue Larraway, Sunnyvale, CA.
Page 106: Noisettines, Laurence Mancini Ilanjian, Taconic, CT.
Page 106: Horns, Helen McGrath, Camarillo, CA.
Page 108: Vinegar Cookies, Winifred Bissonnette, Ludlow, VT.
Page 109: Greek Cinnamon Paximadia, Kathryn Marie Petrofanis, San Pedro, CA.
Page 110: Chocolate Sambuca Cookies, Leslie R. Husted, Clinton, NY.
Page 111: Czechoslovakian Cookies, Barbara Karpin-ski, Somerset, NJ.
Page 111: Hazelnut Cookies, Susan Willey Spalt, Carrboro, NC.
Page 112: Wooden-Spoon Cookies, Cindie David, Lawrenceville, GA.
Page 113: Ricotta-Cheese Cookies, Naoma R. Felt, Bradenton, FL.
Page 114: Cinnamon Twists, Carrie Deegan, Glen Cove, NY.
Page 115: Greek Christmas Cookies, Diane Sanchez, Auburndale, FL.

# Index